The

TEXAS

BED &

BREAKFAST

DIRECTORY

... OVER 500 ALTERNATIVES

Sandra Rinaldo-Watson

Golden Pen Publishing Company
Houston Texas

THE *TEXAS* Bed & Breakfast DIRECTORY

... over 500 alternatives

By Sandra Rinaldo-Watson

Published by:
Golden Pen Publishing Company
P. O. Box 73028
Houston TEXAS 77273-3028 USA
(800) 231-1904

Cover Design by John Cole, Santa Fe NM
Cover Photo by Richard Reynolds, Austin TX
Printed in the United States of America
10 9 8 7 6 5 4 3 2 1

Library of Congress Catalog Card Number
95-76624
ISBN 0-9646258-1-4

The information in this book was supplied in large part by the inns themselves and is subject to change without notice. The author and publisher make no representation that this book is absolutely accurate or complete. Errors and omissions, whether typographical, clerical, or otherwise, may sometimes occur within the book and are unintentional.

INTRODUCTION

A long-standing European tradition, bed and breakfast accommodations in the United States are a relatively recent phenomenon in comparison. Once started down the road, however, we have entered into the industry with good old American enthusiasm and love of free enterprise.

Some bed and breakfasts are historical landmarks, steeped in history, which have been lovingly restored to their former elegance and decorated with wonderful period antiques, and some take on their owner's personality, interests, talents and character in a genuine desire to please the general public. Some offer beautiful country scenes and idyllic vistas, others offer an "oasis" in large cities. Some are rustic and private, and some are quaint and romantic. Some are modern with all the conveniences, and some offer a getaway from telephones, televisions and stress. All offer you genuine Southern Hospitality.

In this book you will find bed and breakfast accommodations for every, and I mean every, possible preference. There are log cabins, mansions, historic landmark homes, tepees, bunkhouses, barns, lake homes, cottages, Sunday houses, lofts, apartments, modern homes, lodges, country inns and working ranches, to name only some of over 500 alternatives.

In the months I have been compiling the information which is contained in this book, I have continually asked the people I have encountered if they had ever stayed at a bed and breakfast. I discovered that only 2% of those asked could answer in the affirmative. Most of them were quickly educated by the author about the wonderful and unique world of bed and breakfasts. Some of those asked were under the impression that bed and breakfasts were for older adults only. Let me dispel that "old wives tale" right now - over two-thirds of the accommodations in this book welcome children - and some are so special that I wish I had children to take there!

While I have made an attempt to give the reader basic information about each bed and breakfast listed in this book, my advice to all is that you ask questions, ask questions and ask more questions. Because this type of accommodation is usually run by the owner, each will have their own rules and restrictions.

Like most things these days, rates also will fluctuate depending on a number of circumstances. The range of rates published for each establishment is meant to give the reader a benchmark and not to state categorically, set in cement rates you will encounter. Most innkeepers require an advance deposit and have cancellation policies which they enforce. Usually the taxes are added to the stated rates, but I have found some who include it in the quoted room rate. Double occupancy rates have been stated in the book for comparison purposes, so be sure to inquire about additional charges for extra guests in a room.

Depending on the size of the bed and breakfast, innkeepers may offer to host small business meetings, weddings, seminars, and retreats. Many B&B's offer discounts for mid week business travelers, senior citizens, extended stays, and for parties wishing to engage the entire accommodation. Choices are many and varied in this industry, and the educated traveler has only to ask questions to find out what is possible.

I have made no attempt to categorize the bed and breakfasts in this book. They are listed alphabetically (except for a few) by city. I made no judgments as to which B&B's would be in the book, nor did I try to rate them in any way. It is my feeling that the traveling public's wants, needs and expectations are far reaching, and that it was not up to me to tell them what they should like or not like.

The opportunity to be in this book was offered to every single establishment I could locate in the State of Texas. There were two criteria which had to be met: First, the rate had to include guest's breakfast, and second, the name of the innkeeper, manager, or owner had to be submitted. Some of the bed and breakfasts chose to place additional information and a photograph in the directory. They were charged a small fee to offset the cost of reproducing the image.

In an attempt to let the reader know what they can expect, these classifications were used as an *example* of the food which will be served:

Continental: Rolls, Juice, Beverage

Cont'l. Plus: Choice of Rolls/Muffins, Juice, Fruit, Dry Cereal and Beverage

Full: Fruit, Juice, Eggs/Omelets, Pancakes/Waffles, Meat, Beverage

Gourmet: Eggs Benedict, Casseroles, Smoked Fish, Breakfast Steaks, Bagels/Lox, Champagne, Imported Coffee/Teas, Juice

OYO: Host leaves breakfast fixings in refrigerator for guests to prepare when they wish.

Many hosts will accommodate the special diets of their guests - again, ask questions, ask questions. I find that one of the nicest features of staying at a bed and breakfast is the hosts' willingness to accommodate most situations within their power.

Bed and breakfast hosts will always respect their guests' wishes to retreat to their appointed room for peace and quiet. However, most hosts will invite you to join them or other guests on the porch, in the parlor, around the fireplace or in another "common" room for conversation over "tea". This is just one of the marvelous features of staying at a bed and breakfast. Not only do you meet some gracious and hospitable innkeepers, but you meet other travelers and have the opportunity to socialize with some fascinating people.

If you have purchased this book, you are probably already a bed and breakfast enthusiast . . or are about to become one! Once you have experienced the pleasurable adventure of staying at this unique type of accommodation, you will never want to stay in another look-alike, impersonal hotel or motel room ever again.

Reservations are of paramount importance at most bed and breakfast establishments in order for hosts to prepare properly for your arrival and for you to reserve the type of room configuration you desire. Weekends and holidays are a busy time especially - so make those reservations as early as possible so you won't be disappointed.

Look for "special" treats and discounts as you go through the book - some hosts have made special offers to purchasers of this book.

It is my greatest hope that this book will help you find that accommodation which suits your taste, your needs and your sweet dreams !

Author's Note:

This book is written with the purpose of attempting to raise the awareness of the traveling public to a wonderful, never-ending variety of alternative lodging, deep in the heart of Texas . . .the exciting world of Bed and Breakfasts.

 **Abilene**

BED & BREAKFAST ABILENE STYLE
4073 Caldwell Road
Abilene 79601
Reservations: 915 677 9677

Innkeeper:	Betty Hood, Resident Owner
Open:	All Year
Facilities:	4 Bedrooms, All Private Baths
Breakfast:	Continental
Rates:	$40 - $150 For 2 Guests
Payment:	Amex,Check

BLUE WILLOW BED & BREAKFAST
435 College Avenue
Abilene 79601
Reservations: 915 677 8420

Innkeeper:	Cindy Deegan, Resident Owner
Open:	All Year
Facilities:	1 Bedroom, 1 Bath Carriage House
Breakfast:	Continental Plus
Rates:	$85 For 2 Guests
Payment:	Check

BOLIN'S PRAIRIE HOUSE BED & BREAKFAST
508 Mulberry
Abilene 79601
Reservations: 915 675 5855

Innkeepers:	Sam & Ginny Bolin, Resident Owners
Open:	All Year
Facilities:	4 Bedrooms, 2 Pvt. Bath, 1 Shared
Breakfast:	Full
Rates:	$50 - $65 For 2 Guests
Payment:	MC,Visa,Amex,Check

 **Albany**

VIRGINIA'S BED & BREAKFAST
310 Breckenridge St
Albany 76430
Reservations: 915 762 2013

Innkeeper:	Virginia Baker, Resident Owner
Open:	All Year
Facilities:	5 Bedrooms, All Private Baths
Breakfast:	Full
Rates:	$50 - $55 For 2 Guests
Payment:	Check

 **Alpine**

THE WHITE HOUSE INN
2003 Fort Davis Hwy
Alpine 79830
Reservations: 915 837 1401

Innkeeper:	Anita Bradney, Resident Owners
Open:	All Year
Facilities:	4 Bedrooms, All Private Baths
Breakfast:	Gourmet
Rates:	$65 - $75 For 2 Guests
Payment:	MC,Visa,Disc,Check

THE CORNER HOUSE CAFE
BED & BREAKFAST

801 East Avenue E
Alpine 79830
Reservations: 915 837 7161

Innkeeper:	Jim Glendinning
	Resident Owner
Open:	All Year
Facilities:	4 Bedrooms
	3 Private Baths, 1 Shared
Breakfast:	Full
Rates:	$60 For 2 Guests
Payment:	MC,Visa,Amex,Check

This substantial brick-built townhome (three stories were built in 1937) is surrounded by trees and lawn. It is located at the corner of US 90 and TX 118, just 80 miles from the Big Bend National Park and 30 miles from the Davis Mountains State Park.

There are four private bedrooms, each able to accommodate two guests and each with its own private bath. Also available is one single bedroom with a shared bath. Additional accommodations are presently under construction.

Breakfast, consisting of four different menus including home baked rolls, is prepared and served between 7 - 9 a.m. Lunch is available Tuesday through Saturday at additional cost. Afternoon tea, snacks and drinks are available upon request.

Scottish-born world traveler and host, Jim Glendinning, specializes in extending travel tips and useful hints to guests, who are greeted with a welcome drink upon arrival. Jim, having written a guide book to the Big Bend Region, is well aware of the great diversity of natural attactions in the region including hiking, camping, birding, rafting and travel to Mexico.

Children and Pets are welcome. Smoking on porch only. Reservations are requested.

Directions: At corner of US 90 & TX 118 (South) to Big Bend. Two blocks from Sul Ross State University. Six blocks from downtown Alpine.

Member: Texas Hotel & Motel Association

 **Alto**

LINCREST LODGE

Highway 21, East
Alto 75925
Reservations: 409 858 2223

Innkeepers:	Chet & Charlene
	Resident Owners
Open:	All Year
Facilities:	6 Bedrooms
	2 Private Baths, 2 Shared
Breakfast:	Full
Rates:	$75 For 2 Guests
Payment:	MC,Visa,Amex,Check

Lincrest Lodge, located on 16 acres just 23 miles west of Nacogdoches, is a Dutch colonial style home with gracious and distinctive lodging and meeting accommodations. The three story structure has over 7,000 sq.ft. and is located on the crest of a hill overlooking the Angelina River Valley. The establishment boasts a marble entrance hall, porch cafe, meeting rooms, individually decorated guest rooms, and a beautifully appointed living and dining room.

Lincrest Lodge hosts, Chet and Charlene, are dedicated to providing guests with a unique, gracious and enjoyable stay in scenic Central East Texas. They have incorporated their own personal history in the design of each suite, offering elegant baths, comfortable beds and a quiet world of your own, some with spectacular views.

Lincrest guests will awaken to the delicious aromas of home cooked breakfast or leaner delicacies, served from 7-9 a.m. The porch cafe is the perfect setting for a deli lunch or guests may arrange for a delightful box lunch to carry on a scenic adventure. After your excursion or a quiet afternoon, refresh yourself with a cafe tea-time served from 4-6 p.m. Follow tea-time with a country buffet, served Wednesday through Saturday 6:00 - 8:00 p.m. Special affairs are catered to suit any group or occasion from seminars to parties.

Smoking is restricted to the deck and patios. Facilities for the handicapped are provided, and pets are not allowed inside of the lodge. Reservations are required. Children over twelve years of age are welcome. Additional third party bed arrangements may be made in advance.

Directions: Hwy 59 or 69 to State Hwy 21 - 4 miles East of the town of Alto.

 **Amarillo**

GALBRAITH HOUSE BED & BREAKFAST
1710 South Polk Street
Amarillo 79102
Reservations: 806 374 0237/800 Nts Polk

Innkeeper:	Martha Shaw, Manager
Open:	All Year
Facilities:	5 Bedrooms, All Private Baths
Breakfast:	Full
Rates:	$85 For 2 Guests
Payment:	All Major,Check

PARKVIEW HOUSE
1311 South Jefferson Street
Amarillo 79101
Reservations: 806 373 9464

Innkeepers:	Carol & Nabil Dia, Resident Owners
Open:	All Year
Facilities:	5 Bedrooms, 1 Pvt. Bath, 2 Shared
Breakfast:	Continental Plus
Rates:	$65 - $85 For 2 Guests
Payment:	MC,Visa,Amex,Check

THE HARRISON HOUSE
1710 South Harrison Street
Amarillo 79102
Reservations: 806 374 1710

Innkeeper:	David Horsley, Resident Owner
Open:	All Year
Facilities:	1 Bedroom, 1 Bath
Breakfast:	Full
Rates:	$55 - $75 For 2 Guests
Payment:	MC,Visa,Check

Anderson

SARAH'S HOUSE BED & BREAKFAST
Main & Woodward
Anderson 77830
Reservations: 409 873 2809

Innkeepers:	Joanne & Bill Minsky
	Resident Owners
Open:	Seasonal 4/15 To 10/31
Facilities:	1 Bedroom, 1 Bath Cottage
Breakfast:	Continental
Rates:	$75 For 2 Guests
Payment:	Check

Archer City

SPUR HOTEL BED & BREAKFAST
110 N. Center
Archer City 76351
Reservations: 817 574 2501

Innkeeper:	Besia Green, Manager
Open:	All Year
Facilities:	11 Bedrooms, All Private Baths
Breakfast:	Continental
Rates:	$56 For 2 Guests
Payment:	Visa,Check

 **Argyle**

ROADRUNNER FARM

14 Fincher Road
Argyle 76226
Reservations: 817 455 2942

Innkeeper:	Jan Michie, Resident Owner
Open:	All Year
Facilities:	2 Bedrooms, All Private Baths
Breakfast:	Gourmet
Rates:	$70 - $80 For 2 Guests
Payment:	Check

10

Located on 32 secluded, gently rolling acres of Horse Country, gracious Texas hospitality can be found by travelers at Roadrunner Farm Bed & Breakfast. A Texas limestone house (featured in "Southern Living"), this bed and breakfast is just minutes from Denton.

Guests are invited to play a game of horseshoes in the back yard, go for a dip in the pool to cool off, go "creek walking" or hiking on the wooded trails. It's very relaxing to sit on the veranda with a cup of coffee, iced tea, or a margarita and watch the horses grazing or sit by a toasty fire in the winter. Among other things, your hostess Jan Michie runs a boarding stable, trains horses and competes in a sport called "eventing". Says Jan, "I love my place and like to share it with others". She is very conversant with happenings in this area and would be happy to give you tour information.

The accommodations include two spacious bedrooms with private baths. A gourmet country breakfast is served to guests. "Girls Night Out", rehearsal dinners, wedding, birthday and anniversary parties are right up her alley. Or perhaps you are interested in a hayride, a weekend retreat or a company get together.

There are designated areas for smoking. Children who are six or older are welcome. The home cannot accommodate pets. Lunch and/or dinner are available upon request. Reservations are preferred. A 15% discount is offered to guests who stay a week. Snacks and drinks are provided.

Directions: Take 35E from Dallas, North to S.H. 407, West to Bartonville Store. Turn Right and follow 407 to Left on Fincher Rd. Go .25 miles to Farm.

 **Athens**

CARRIAGE HOUSE AT HICKORY HILL

Fm 753, Rt 2, Box 2153
Athens 75751
Reservations: 903 677 3939/800 808-Beds

Innkeepers:	Larry & Carol Kelly, Resident Owners
Open:	All Year
Facilities:	3 Bedrooms, All Private Baths
Breakfast:	Full
Rates:	$85 - $110 For 2 Guests
Payment:	MC, Visa, Check

DUNSAVAGE FARMS B&B

Box 176
Athens 75751
Reservations: 800 225 6982

Innkeeper:	Lyn Dunsavage, Resident Owner
Open:	All Year
Facilities:	5 Bedrooms, All Private Baths
Breakfast:	Full
Rates:	$79.95 For 2 Guests
Payment:	MC, Visa, Amex, Check

GERANIUM HOUSE BED & BREAKFAST

518 E. Tyler
Athens 75751
Reservations: 903 675 3317

Innkeeper:	Ralph Anderson, Resident Owner
Open:	All Year
Facilities:	5 Bedrooms, 2 Shared Baths
Breakfast:	Full
Rates:	$45 - $75 For 2 Guests
Payment:	MC, Visa, Check

Aubrey

THE GUEST HOUSE
Hwy 377 N
Aubrey 76227
Reservations: 817 440 2076

Innkeeper:	Lynne Weil, Resident Owner
Open:	All Year
Facilities:	3 Bedrooms, Pvt Baths
	Plus 2 Bed-1bath Cottage
Breakfast:	Continental Plus
Rates:	$55 - $85 For 2 Guests
Payment:	Amex,Check

Austin

AUNT DOLLY'S ATTIC B&B
12023 Rotherham Drive
Austin 78753
Reservations: 512 837 5320

Innkeeper:	Mary Ralan, Resident Owner
Open:	All Year
Facilities:	2 Bedrooms, 1 Shared Bath
Breakfast:	Continental
Rates:	$65 For 2 Guests
Payment:	Check

AUSTIN WILDFLOWER INN

1200 W. 21-1/2 Street
Austin 78705
Reservations: 512 477 9639

Innkeeper:	Kay Jackson, Resident Owner
Open:	All Year
Facilities:	4 Bedrooms, 2 Pvt Baths, 1 Shared
Breakfast:	Full
Rates:	$59 - $75 For 2 Guests
Payment:	MC,Visa,Check

CARRINGTON'S BLUFF BED & BREAKFAST

1900 David Street
Austin 78705
Reservations: 512 479 0638

Innkeepers:	Gwen & David Fullbrook
	Resident Owners
Open:	All Year
Facilities:	8 Bedrooms, 6 Pvt Baths, 1 Shared
Breakfast:	Full
Rates:	$50 - $89 For 2 Guests
Payment:	All Major,Check

CITIVIEW BED & BREAKFAST

1405 E. Riverside Drive
Austin 78741
Reservations: 512 441 2606

Innkeeper:	Carol Hayden, Manager
Open:	All Year
Facilities:	3 Bedrooms, All Private Baths
Breakfast:	Full
Rates:	$109 - $139 For 2 Guests
Payment:	All Major, Check

FAIRVIEW -
A Bed & Breakfast Establishment
1304 Newning Avenue
Austin 78704
Reservations: 512 444 4746

Innkeepers:	Duke & Nancy Waggoner, Res. Owner
Open:	All Year
Facilities:	6 Bedrooms, All Private Baths
Breakfast:	Full
Rates:	$89 - $129 For 2 Guests
Payment:	All Major, Check

GOVERNOR'S INN BED & BREAKFAST
611 West 22 Street
Austin 78705
Reservations: 512 477 0711

Innkeepers:	Gwen & David Fullbrook, Res.Owners
Open:	All Year
Facilities:	10 Bedrooms, All Private Baths
Breakfast:	Full
Rates:	$49 - $99 For 2 Guests
Payment:	All Major,Check

MARSHALL RANCH BED & BREAKFAST
19210 Austin Blvd
Austin 78645
Reservations: 512 267 9642

Innkeeper:	Valerie Ambroson, Resident Owner
Open:	All Year
Facilities:	Two 1 Bedroom-1 Bath Guest Houses
Breakfast:	Full
Rates:	$125 - $175 For 2 Guests
Payment:	Check

LAKE TRAVIS BED & BREAKFAST

4446 Eck Lane
Austin 78734
Reservations: 512 266 3386/800 484 9095

Innkeepers:	Judy & Vic Dwyer
	Resident Owners
Open:	All Year
Facilities:	3 Bedrooms, All Private Baths
Breakfast:	Continental Plus In Bed
Rates:	$110 - $125 For 2 Guests
Payment:	MC,Visa,Amex,Check

Lake Travis Bed & Breakfast, a unique waterfront retreat hanging over a cliff with an expansive view of 50 miles is the setting for an adult luxurious getaway.

The natural beauty of the surroundings are reflected in the seven level native limestone house with Southwest furnishings and sculptures. Each of the three guest bedrooms have panoramic lake views, private baths with gold fixtures and a deck overlooking the lake.

It's just steps to the water and a floating marina with docking facilities, kitchen, bar, dining area and sun deck on top. Mini-resort better describes the amenities: Pool with water table, spa, steam sauna, fishing, swimming and sunning. On-site massage is available, and there are nearby boat and jet ski rentals, golf, tennis, horseback riding, hiking, vintage steam train trips and cave exploration.

Inside you'll find a two story stone fireplace, pool table, gameroom and library with video movies. With ten decks strategically located around the property and lake, privacy is assured. Begin the day with a gourmet continental breakfast in bed, or on your deck where you can watch the birds soar and sailboats drift along.

Dine at one of the famous gourmet restaurants and return to a romantic setting of the moon and lights dancing on the water, the subtle night sounds and a star-filled sky. You'll know that you've found a piece of heaven at Lake Travis Bed & Breakfast.

Smoking and pets are not allowed. Reservations are required. Afternoon tea is served. Check in time is 3-6 p.m. and check out is at 12 noon.

Directions: 1.5 miles west of Mansfield Dam, turn North toward lake on Eck and continue 1 mile to the blue iron gate.

Member: Professional Assn of Innkeepers Int'l

MEDWAY RANCH

13500 Pecan Drive
Austin 78734
Reservations: 512 263 5151

Innkeepers:	Todd Prather, Manager
Open:	All Year
Facilities:	3 Bedrooms Main House
	3 Cabins and a Bunkhouse
Breakfast:	Full
Rates:	$65 - $100 Per Person
Payment:	Check

Surrounded by 6,000 primitive acres in the Texas Hill Country, Medway Ranch has the space and facilities to custom design any party or event that your heart and pocketbook desire.

An expansive Hacienda on Lake Austin, this ranch is the formal venue for weddings, receptions, dinners, breakfasts or get-away executive meetings. Oversized fireplaces, exquisite carving and paneling from the old New York Stock Exchange, a banquet-size dinner table and a magnificent Steinway grand piano provide a sophisticated, yet relaxed, ambiance for any occasion.

The Hacienda has three guest rooms for tradi-tional bed and breakfast travelers. Three cabins and a bunkhouse are available for retreats and weekend gatherings. Guests receive a full country breakfast each morning.

Outdoors there is plenty of ground for tents and dance floors for receptions and events. Or Hoe Down and chow down to Texas tunes and Texas barbecue in the large pavilion. Bonfires and coun-tryside hayrides often complete the evening. Com-pany, church or school picnics have space to breathe in the meadows for baseball, football or three-legged races.

The new sports court provides for tennis, shuf-fleboard and basketball, while the sanded volleyball court is a serious consideration for the highly com-petitive, and what is an afternoon in the country without a trail-ride or old fashioned game of croquet or horseshoes?

Your host, Todd Prather, will help you create an unforgettable memory of Medway Ranch.

Reservations are required. Smoking and pets are not allowed.

PEACEFUL HILL BED & BREAKFAST
6401 River Place Blvd.
Austin 78730
Reservations: 512 338 1817

Innkeeper:	Peninnah Thurmond, Resident Owner
Open:	All Year
Facilities:	2 Bedrooms, All Private Baths
Breakfast:	Full
Rates:	$60 - $65 For 2 Guests
Payment:	MC,Visa,Amex,Check

PEARL STREET INN
1809 Pearl Street
Austin 78701
Reservations: 512 477 2233

Innkeeper:	J. Bickford, Resident Owner
Open:	All Year
Facilities:	5 Bedrooms, All Private Baths
Breakfast:	Continental Plus
Rates:	$100 - $115 For 2 Guests
Payment:	All Major,Check

PICKEL'S LAKE TRAVIS BED & BREAKFAST
8010 Lakeview St
Austin 78641
Reservations: 512 331 8733/800 323 3737

Innkeeper:	Gerry Cowna, Resident Owner
Open:	All Year
Facilities:	4 Bedrooms, All Private Baths
Breakfast:	Full
Rates:	$60 - $95 For 2 Guests
Payment:	MC,Visa,Amex

SOUTHARD HOUSE BED & BREAKFAST

908 Blanco
Austin 78703
Reservations: 512 474 4731

Innkeepers:	Jerry & Rejina Southard
	Resident Owners
Open:	All Year
Facilities:	11 Bedrooms, All Private Baths
Breakfast:	Full & Continental Plus
Rates:	$59 - $129 For 2 Guests
Payment:	All Major,Check

THE BREMOND HOUSE

404 West 7th Street
Austin 78701
Reservations: 512 482 0411

Innkeeper:	Vicki Bell, Resident Owner
Open:	All Year
Facilities:	4 Bedrooms, 2 Pvt Baths,1 Shared
Breakfast:	Full
Rates:	$84 - $104 For 2 Guests
Payment:	MC,Visa,Amex

THE CHEQUERED SHADE BED & BREAKFAST

2530 Pearce Road
Austin 78730
Reservations: 512 346 8318/800 577 5786

Innkeeper:	Millie Scott, Resident Owner
Open:	All Year
Facilities:	3 Bedrooms, 2 Pvt Baths, 1 Shared
Breakfast:	Full
Rates:	$55 - $75 For 2 Guests
Payment:	MC,Visa,Amex

609 W. 33rd Street
Austin 78705
Reservations: 512 459 0534

Innkeepers:	Barbara Love & David Wells, Resident Owners
Open:	All Year
Facilities:	5 Bedrooms, All Private Baths
Breakfast:	Full
Rates:	$55 - $79 For 2 Guests
Payment:	All Major,Check

Circa 1922, The Brook House, surrounded by tall oaks, has been lovingly restored to an appealing blend of old world charm and modern conveniences. Located near the University of Texas campus, the main house has large square rooms.

The yard hosts a large tin-roofed gazebo, herb and flower gardens and provides a haven within the city for weary travelers. Hosts Barbara and David extend wonderful hospitality.

Antique-filled rooms, high ceilings and original windows are just part of this home's charm. The Blue Room has an elevated mahogany Queen size four-poster bed, antique dresser, original light fixture, antique rocker and a screened porch shaded by a century-old Spanish oak. The Rose Room, named for the small stained glass window in the bathroom, has an antique pine King size bed, lacy curtains and antique claw foot tub.

Across the backyard, the Carriage House has its own separate entrance for privacy, kitchen facilities, dormer windows, antique furnishings and a Queen size iron bed and Queen sleeper sofa. The "Cottage" also with a private entrance, boasts an antique oak table and chairs, antique oak Queen size bed, day bed/trundle and kitchen facilities.

Breakfast delights, flavored with fresh herbs from Barbara's garden, are served outside on the greenery-lined veranda, weather permitting or in the dining room.

Smoking is allowed on outside porch and grounds only. Small pets will be accommodated in the cottage only. Children are welcome. Reservations are required. Check in is at 2 p.m. and check out at 12 noon.

THE MC CALLUM HOUSE

613 W. 32nd Street
Austin 78705
Reservations: 512 451 6744

Innkeepers:	Nancy & Roger Danley
	Resident Owners
Open:	All Year
Facilities:	5 Bedrooms, All Private Baths
Breakfast:	Full
Rates:	$55 - $99 For 1 Guest
Payment:	MC,Visa,Check

TRAILS END BED & BREAKFAST

12223 Trails End Rd
Austin 78641
Reservations: 512 267 2901

Innkeeper:	Jo Ann Patty, Resident Owner
Open:	All Year
Facilities:	2 Bedrooms With Pvt Baths
	2 Bed-1bath Guest House
Breakfast:	Full
Rates:	$65 - $95 For 2 Guests
Payment:	MC,Visa,Amex,Check

TRIPLE CREEK GUEST RANCH

16301 Fitzhugh Road
Austin 78736
Reservations: 512 264 1371/800 214 1371

Innkeeper:	Nola Fowler, Resident Owner
Open:	All Year
Facilities:	4 Bedrooms, All Private Baths
Breakfast:	Full (all meals in price)
Rates:	$175 For 2 Guests
Payment:	MC,Visa,Disc

WOODBURN HOUSE BED & BREAKFAST

4401 Avenue D
Austin 78751
Reservations: 512 458 4335

Innkeepers:	Herb & Sandra Dickson
	Resident Owners
Open:	All Year
Facilities:	4 Bedrooms, All Private Baths
Breakfast:	Gourmet
Rates:	$75 - $85 For 2 Guests
Payment:	Check

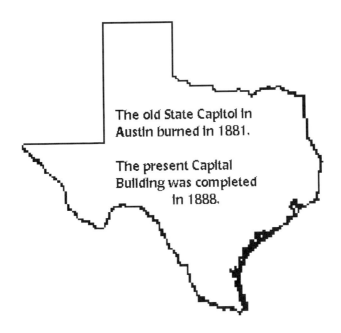

The old State Capitol in
Austin burned in 1881.

The present Capital
Building was completed
in 1888.

ZILLER HOUSE

800 Edgecliff Terrace
Austin 78704
Reservations: 512 462 0100/800 949 5446

Innkeepers:	Sam Kindred and Wendy Sandberg, Resident Owners
Open:	All Year
Facilities:	3 Bedrooms, 1 Suite Carriage House All Private Baths
Breakfast:	Gourmet OYO
Rates:	$90 - $110 For 2 Guests
Payment:	MC,Visa,Amex,Check

Ziller House built in 1938 is a gated, secluded estate on the cliff above the bank of Town Lake. Surrounded by 2.5 acres of foliage, this 8,000 sq.ft. Mediterranean style mansion is a beautiful country home, with the city far away. Although the home is thoroughly modern, the sophisticated Ziller House has a historical feel with its intricate architectural details, huge limestone fireplace and elegant furnishings.

The rooms, three of which are upstairs, have their own personalities. The Library Room is lined with bookshelves and offers a pretty view of the Lake. The Balcony Room is surrounded on all sides by live oaks, and the Sun Suite boasts a canopy bed and separate sitting area (with sleeper sofa).

Each room has its own tiled private bath with tub and shower, and the amenities include color TV with cable, private portable phones, coffee/tea maker, linens and tableware. The home has an open, comfortable living room, an elegant dining room and a wine tasting room. The grounds (which serve as the smoking area of the Ziller estate), include a gazebo terrace and Jacuzzi spa.

A gourmet breakfast (cooked on an enormous Wolf stove) is tucked away in a small refrigerator that is in each room's service cabinet.

Check in time is 4-10 p.m. with variations by prior arrangement. Check out time is 1:00 p.m. Ask about corporate and extended stay rates. Children and pets are welcome

Directions: Take Riverside Drive exit from IH-35, travel West to first intersection and turn right onto Travis Heights which will dead end. Turn left onto Edgecliff Terrace and follow it to its conclusion at the estate.

 # Avinger

MC KENZIE MANOR

Route 1, Box 440
Avinger 75630
Reservations: 903 755 2240/903 755 9648

Innkeepers:	Fred & Anne Mc Kenzie
	Resident Owners
Open:	All Year
Facilities:	10 Bedrooms
	8 Private Baths
	1 Shared Bath
Breakfast:	Full
Rates:	$65 - $95 For 2 Guests
Payment:	MC,Visa,Check

Escape to the privacy of this spacious, rustic, rock lodge set on the shores of beautiful Lake O'the Pines, 17 miles West of Jefferson in Avinger. McKenzie Manor is an East Texas rock manor with country and antique furnishings nestled in a natural pine and hardwood forest with native plants, animals and birds. Sit on the wide decks and watch eagles soar, beavers build dams and deer graze. Walk the nature trails exploring the private ponds and native foliage.

Experience beautiful sunrises and sunsets and listen for the crickets, frogs and whippoorwills to lull you to sleep. Relax in the gazebo or by the large rock fireplace with a good book from the private library of your host, Historian and Published Author, Fred McKenzie.

This lake front lodge is a four generation family home, designed with a large meeting room, vaulted ceilings, and stained glass windows. The bedrooms are spacious with private entrances, balconies, ceiling fans and private baths. All rooms are adjacent to sitting areas, each decorated in its own unique style with lovely antiques and family possessions.

Amenities include hot tub, complimentary refreshments, access to kitchen, meeting facilities and a private 3000 foot airstrip. The Manor will accommodate retreats, receptions and weddings. Arrangements for catering, canoeing and boat tours are handled by your hosts.

Smoking is allowed on the decks only. No arrangements for pets. Check in time is 2 p.m. and check out time is 12 noon. Reservations are required.

Directions: On north shore of Lake O'the Pines. Highway 729.

Ballinger

MIZ VIRGINIA'S BED & BREAKFAST
IN THE OLD PARK HOTEL
Courthouse Square
Ballinger 76821
Reservations: 800 344 0781

Innkeepers:	S.C. & Juanita Chrisco
	Resident Owners
Open:	All Year
Facilities:	7 Bedrooms, 3 Pvt Baths,4 Shared
Breakfast:	Full
Rates:	$38 - $65 For 2 Guests
Payment:	All Major, Check

Bandera

BACKYARD BUNKHOUSE
Rt. 3, Box 1, Hwy #173
Bandera 78003
Reservations: 210 796 3430

Innkeeper:	Jan McCollum, Resident Owner
Open:	All Year
Facilities:	1 Bedroom, 1 Bath
Breakfast:	OYO
Rates:	$55 For 2 Guests
Payment:	Check

BANDERA CREEK BED & BREAKFAST

P.O. Box 964
Bandera 78003
Reservations: 210 460 3517

Innkeeper:	Gay Guilott, Resident Owner
Open:	All Year
Facilities:	2 Bedrooms, 1 Bath
Breakfast:	Continental Plus
Rates:	$85 - $105 For 4 Guests
Payment:	MC,Visa,Check

COOL WATER ACRES

Rt. 1, Box 785
Bandera 78003
Reservations: 210 796 4866

Innkeepers:	John & Julie Dinse, Resident Owners
Open:	All Year
Facilities:	1 Bedroom, 1 Bath
	Plus 1 Bed-1bath Cabin
Breakfast:	Inquire
Rates:	$50 - $70 For 2 Guests
Payment:	Check

DIAMOND H BED & BREAKFAST

Highway 16 North
Bandera 78003
Reservations: 210 796 4820

Innkeepers:	Polly & Tom Herrington
	Resident Owners
Open:	All Year
Facilities:	7 Bedrooms, All Private Baths
Breakfast:	Full
Rates:	$50 - $95 Per Room
Payment:	MC,Visa,Check

HACKBERRY LODGE BED & BREAKFAST
1005 Hackberry
Bandera 78003
Reservations: 210 460 7134

Innkeeper:	Janice Kuykendall, Resident Owner
Open:	All Year
Facilities:	9 Bedrooms, All Private Baths
Breakfast:	Continental
Rates:	$60 - $135 For 2 Guests
Payment:	MC,Visa,Check

HORSESHOE INN
Rt. 3, Box 300
Bandera 78003
Reservations: 210 796 3105/800 352 3810

Innkeeper:	Patricia Moore, Resident Owner
Open:	All Year
Facilities:	7 Bedrooms, All Private Baths
Breakfast:	Full
Rates:	$40 - $50 For 2 Guests
Payment:	MC, Visa,Check

RICOCHET RANCH BED & BREAKFAST
#55 Robin Dale Road
Bandera 78003
Reservations: 210 460 7500

Innkeeper:	Janice Kuykendall, Resident Owner
Open:	All Year
Facilities:	Three 1 Bedroom-1 Bath Cottages
Breakfast:	Continental
Rates:	$52 - $85 For 2 Guests
Payment:	MC,Visa,Check

 **Bartlett**

ROBBIE NELL'S COUNTRY INN B&B

540 W. Clark
Bartlett 76511
Reservations: 817 527 4515

Innkeepers:	Robbie & Ken Ritchie
	Resident Owners
Open:	All Year
Facilities:	3 Bedrooms, 2 Shared Baths
Breakfast:	Continental
Rates:	$45 - $55 For 2 Guests
Payment:	Check

 **Beaumont**

GRAND DUERR MANOR

2298 Mc Faddin
Beaumont 77701
Reservations: 409 833 9600

Innkeeper:	Doug Durerr, Resident Owner
Open:	All Year
Facilities:	4 Bedrooms, All Private Baths
Breakfast:	Continental Plus
Rates:	$89 - $149 For 2 Guests
Payment:	Disc, Check

 **Bellville**

BANNER FARM BED & BREAKFAST

8 Mi. East Of Town On FM 331
Bellville 77418
Reservations: 409 865 8534

Innkeeper:	Toni Trimble, Resident Owner
Open:	Seasonal 3/1 To 10/31
Facilities:	3 Bedrooms, 1 Shared Bath
Breakfast:	Full
Rates:	$50 For 2 Guests
Payment:	Check

TOWNSQUARE INN BED & BREAKFAST

21 S. Bell
Bellville 77418
Reservations: 409 865 9021

Innkeepers:	Deborah & Bob Nolen
	Owner/Managers
Open:	All Year
Facilities:	9 Bedrooms, 6 Pvt Baths, Some Shared
Breakfast:	Continental
Rates:	$50 For 2 Guests
Payment:	MC,Visa,Amex,Check

Ben Wheeler

WILD BRIAR COUNTRY INN

P.O. Box 21
Ben Wheeler 75754
Reservations: 903 852 3975

Innkeepers:	Max & Mary Scott, Resident Owners
Open:	All Year
Facilities:	6 Bedrooms, All Private Baths
Breakfast:	Full
Rates:	$100 For 2 Guests
Payment:	Check

Big Sandy

ANNIE'S BED & BREAKFAST

Highway 155 North
Big Sandy 75755
Reservations: 903 636 4355

Innkeepers:	Clifton & Kathy Shaw, Managers
Open:	All Year
Facilities:	12 Bedrooms, 7 Pvt Baths, 3 Shared
Breakfast:	Full
Rates:	$50 - $115 For 2 Guests
Payment:	All Major, Check

 **Blanco**

CREEKWOOD COUNTRY INN

Fall Creek Rd, CR 411
Blanco 78606
Reservations: 210 833 2248

Innkeeper:	Charlotte Dorsey
	Resident Owner
Open:	All Year
Facilities:	2 Bedrooms, All Private Baths
Breakfast:	Gourmet
Rates:	$75 - $85 For 2 Guests
Payment:	Check

Overlooking a spring-fed creek and a wooded bluff, Creekwood Country Inn beckons its guests to sit on the shaded porch and commune with nature at its finest. Guests may roam the six plus acres that are part of this bed and breakfast.

Hostess Charlotte Dorsey, a former city dweller who longed for the peace and tranquillity of the country, believes she has found the perfect place for her in the community of Blanco (population 1,265). She now shares her discovery with guests who want a county getaway where they can relax, watch the wildlife which wanders by, enjoy the brilliant wild-flowers, or take a drive toward San Marcos along "The Devil's Backbone".

There are two bedrooms, one King size and one Queen size, each with its own bath. The decor is art-ful and tasteful creating a warm, comfortable at-mosphere for visitors. Both rooms have French doors and lots of windows to enjoy the scenery.

The gourmet breakfast includes a variety of homemade breads and fresh fruits. Charlotte offers her guests the luxury of special dietary needs, so just be sure to tell her your requirements when you make your reservation. She will also provide you with a picnic lunch upon request at an additional charge. Snacks and beverages are complimentary.

Smoking is limited to outdoors, and pets are not allowed. Handicap accessible. Reservations are re-quired. Discount offered for a two or more night stay.

Directions: Highway 281 to East on CR 411 to third gate on right hand side of road.

OUR HAUS BED & BREAKFAST

508 4th Street
Blanco 78606
Reservations: 210 843 4116

Innkeepers:	Bill & Kelly Silvernail
	Resident Owners
Open:	All Year
Facilities:	2 Bedrooms, All Private Baths
Breakfast:	Full
Rates:	Call Owner For Rate
Payment:	MC, Visa,Check

Our Haus is a Greek revival structure, the oldest part of the house dating back to approximately 1864. The home was owned by Catherine Brown in the late 1800's. In 1871, she began the Blanco Hotel and Livery Stable on this site. An ad from the Blanco Country News dated December 12, 1876 reads, "This house has been nicely refitted and rearranged. Visitors are assured that nothing will be left undone that will lead to the comfort of their guests". You can relax on the porch and enjoy the leisure pace of a small town or visit some of the nearby attractions.

The new owners, Bill and Kelly Silvernail, feel the same way. They purchased the house in 1993 and began restoring the structure for a bed and breakfast. The Silvernails strived to keep the house in as much of its original state as possible. It has antique furnishings, and in the kitchen is Kelly's pride and joy, a 1930's O'Keefe & Merit stove, on which she prepares her favorite breakfast dishes for you to enjoy in the comfortable dining room.

There are two rooms for guests, the Victorian Rose Room and the Country Wildflower Room. Both rooms have a Queen sized bed, private bath and a sitting room.

Smoking is permitted outside. The bed and breakfast is not able to accommodate children or pets. Reservations are required. Check in time is 3 p.m. and check out is at 1 p.m. Ask about off season rates (January 1 - March 1). Special rates are offerred if both rooms are rented by the same party or for extended stays.

Directions: Located ½ block from intersection of Hwy281 and RR 1623, on 4th Street.

Member: Blanco Chamber of Commerce, Old Blanco Merchants and Business Association.

 **Bluff Dale**

THE HIDEAWAY
COUNTRY LOG CABINS

Rt 2, Box 148
Bluff Dale 76433
Reservations: 817 823 6606

Innkeepers:	Larry & Marjo Skiles
	Resident Owners
Open:	All Year
Facilities:	Three 1 Bedroom-1 Bath Cabins
Breakfast:	Continental Plus OYO
Rates:	$69 - $93 For 2 Guests
Payment:	Check

If you need to get away from it all, you've found the place....The Hideaway Cabins! This bed and breakfast is a secluded country retreat offering complete privacy to its guests. Three rustic cabins lie hidden among the oaks, surrounded by 155 acres of peace and quiet, just a short drive from Dallas/Ft. Worth. You can fish in one of the ponds, hike in the woods, star gaze from your hot tub or just relax with a good book. For the somewhat more active guest, equipment is available for volleyball, badminton, horseshoes, and there's room for target shooting, too.

The rustic Log Cabin is a spacious, one room lodge pole pine hideout. A four-poster bed and hide-a-bed sofa sleep four comfortably. There's a screened porch, a sundeck and hot tub. The Line-shack, built of pine and spruce logs, sleeps four, and features a bedroom with double bed and a living area with trundle daybed, full carpeting and central heat/air. The bath has a shower only, but there's an outdoor hot tub. The Cedars accommodates seven guests and has a roomy loft with a beautiful view and full bath. A fireplace warms the living area which opens onto your private deck and hot tub.

For breakfast, you can choose a continental plus style with delicious breads and muffins, cold cereals and fresh fruits, or they will stock the refrigerator with the makings, and you can cook your own hot breakfast .

Smoking is permitted. Children under twelve stay free. Reservations are required. Pets are welcome . . . you can even bring your own horse. Discount for three or more nights. Special gift for honeymoon, anniversary or birthday guests.

Member: Texas Hotel/Motel Association

 # Boerne

BORGMAN'S SUNDAY HOUSE
911 South Main
Boerne 78006
Reservations: 210 249 9563/800 633 7339

Innkeepers:	Mike & Mary Jewell, Managers
Open:	All Year
Facilities:	13 Bedrooms, All Private Baths
Breakfast:	Full
Rates:	$48 - $70 For 2 Guests
Payment:	All Major,Check

 # Brenham

ANT STREET INN
107 W. Commerce
Brenham 77833
Reservations: 409 836 7393

Innkeepers:	Tommy & Pam Traylor
	Resident Owners
Open:	All Year
Facilities:	13 Bedrooms, All Private Baths
Breakfast:	Full
Rates:	$85 - $160 For 2 Guests
Payment:	MC,Visa,Check

CAMPBELL'S COUNTRY HOME
BED & BREAKFAST
7752 Marcus Road
Brenham 77833
Reservations: 409 830 0278

Innkeepers:	Jim & Chris Campbell, Resident Owners
Open:	All Year
Facilities:	2 Bedrooms, All Private Baths
Breakfast:	Full
Rates:	$75 For 2 Guests
Payment:	MC,Visa,Check

CAPTAIN CLAY HOME BED & BREAKFAST
FM 390
Brenham 77833
Reservations: 409 836 1916

Innkeeper:	Thelma Zwiener, Resident Owner
Open:	All Year
Facilities:	4 Bedrooms, 2 Pvt Baths, 2 Shared
Breakfast:	Full
Rates:	$50 - $75 For 2 Guests
Payment:	Check

COTTONTAIL INN BED & BREAKFAST
Rt. 4, Box 367
Brenham 77833
Reservations: 409 836 9485

Innkeepers:	Eileen & Ludwig Wuycheck Resident Owners
Open:	All Year
Facilities:	2 Bedrooms, All Private Baths
Breakfast:	Full
Rates:	Call Innkeeper
Payment:	Check

DEWBERRY HILL BED & BREAKFAST

Meyer Lane & Randerman Rd
Brenham 77834
Reservations: 409 836 6879

Innkeepers:	Peter & Cynthia Nauman
	Resident Owners
Open:	All Year
Facilities:	2 Bedrooms, Pvt Baths
	Plus 1 Bed-1bath Apt
Breakfast:	Gourmet
Rates:	$75 - $85 For 2 Guests
Payment:	Check

FAR VIEW BED & BREAKFAST

1804 South Park Street
Brenham 77833
Reservations: 409 836 1672

Innkeepers:	David & Tonya Meyer
	Resident Owner
Open:	All Year
Facilities:	5 Bedrooms, All Private Baths
Breakfast:	Full
Rates:	$85 - $115 For 2 Guests
Payment:	MC,Visa,Check

HEARTLAND COUNTRY INN

Palestine Rd, Cr 68
Brenham 77833
Reservations: 409 836 1864

Innkeeper:	Shirley Sacks, Resident Owner
Open:	All Year
Facilities:	18 Bedrooms, 14 Shared Baths
Breakfast:	Full
Rates:	$60 - $90 For 2 Guests
Payment:	Check

MOCKINGBIRD HILL BED & BREAKFAST

Baranowski Rd, Rt 3, Box 88
Brenham 77833
Reservations: 409 836 5329

Innkeepers:	Tom & Ann McGraw, Resident Owners
Open:	All Year
Facilities:	7 Bedrooms, 5 Pvt Baths, 2 Shared
Breakfast:	Gourmet
Rates:	$75 - $100 For 2 Guests
Payment:	Check

NUECES CANYON BED & BREAKFAST

9501 U.S. 290 W
Brenham 77833
Reservations: 409 289 5600/800 925 5058

Innkeepers:	Beverly & George Caloudas Resident Owners
Open:	All Year
Facilities:	3 Bedrooms, 1 Pvt Bath, 1 Shared
Breakfast:	Continental Plus
Rates:	$75 - $90 For 2 Guests
Payment:	MC,Visa,Amex,Check

THE BRENHAM HOUSE

705 Clinton Street
Brenham 77833
Reservations: 409 830 0477/800 259 8367

Innkeepers:	David & Janice Phillips Resident Owners
Open:	All Year
Facilities:	3 Bedrooms, All Private Baths
Breakfast:	Full
Rates:	$80 For 2 Guests
Payment:	Amex, Disc, Check

MARIPOSA RANCH
BED & BREAKFAST

La Bahia Road, Rt. 4, Box 172
Brenham 77833
Reservations: 409 836 4545/409 836 4712

Innkeepers:	Johnna & Charles Chamberlain
	Resident Owners
Open:	All Year
Facilities:	9 Bedrooms
	7 Private Baths, 2 Shared
Breakfast:	Gourmet
Rates:	$65 - $150 For 2 Guests
Payment:	MC, Visa, Check

The main house of this bed and breakfast, a 100 year old Texas Plantation home, sits atop an oak-covered hill with a breathtaking view of the quiet rolling country side. The house has been completely renovated and is one of the grandest places in this part of the country, with its old-fashioned charm and elegance, coupled with all the modern conveniences you will come to expect at Mariposa Ranch.

In the main house you may choose from two rooms, Brazos and Tejas, each with twelve foot ceilings, tastefully decorated with fine period antiques, each with private bath. Then there's the Texas Ranger Cabin, a frontier log cabin, completely renovated to maintain its rustic pioneer charm, including a large stone fireplace with hook & crane, Queen sleeper sofa, TV, microwave, refrigerator, large bath with red claw foot tub and a loft upstairs with a Queen bed. This cabin, dedicated to the Texas Rangers in October 1994, overlooks the Yegua Valley with panoramic views.

There's also the original 100 year old ranch-house homestead, the Reinauer Guest House. It offers three bedrooms, two baths, full kitchen, fireplace and is furnished with cozy antiques. Or you may choose Fern Oaks Cottage, a charming accommodation with its own kitchenette, bath and fireplace. Check out Dr. Red's House, a two-story 165 year old Texas Plantation home, each floor containing a luxurious suite, with two fireplaces in each suite.

A country breakfast is served Friday - Sunday. A continental breakfast is served during the week. Reservations are required. Mid-week discounts except during Bluebonnet season.

Broaddus

SAM RAYBURN LAKE BED & BREAKFAST
Wood Village Addn, Rt 1, Box 258
Broaddus 75929
Reservations: 409 872 3666

Innkeepers:	Jean & Gene Cole, Resident Owners
Open:	All Year
Facilities:	3 Bedroom, 1 Bath Cottage
Breakfast:	Continental Plus
Rates:	$55 For 2 Guests
Payment:	Check

Buchanan Dam

MYSTIC COVE BED & BREAKFAST
Rt 1, Box 309B
Buchanan Dam 78609
Reservations: 512 793 6642

Innkeepers:	Loretta & Ralph Dueweke
	Resident Owners
Open:	All Year
Facilities:	2 Bedrooms,Private Baths
	Plus 1Bed-1bath Guest House
Breakfast:	Full
Rates:	$65 - $135 For 2 Guests
Payment:	Check

SPINDLETOP

Derived from the shape of a nearby tree, Spindeltop was the name given the famous Lucas Gusher that came in January 10, 1901, at Big Hill in Jefferson County, near Beaumont. At the level of 1,160 feet, after an initial spurt, the gusher broke loose with a roar, spewing over 900,000 barrels of oil onto the ground before the well could be capped. The lake of oil remained for several weeks until it was ignited from the sparks of a passing train and partially burned.

Although the first oil was discovered in Texas in 1543 by Luis de Moscoso, who used seepage from oil springs near Sabine Pass as caulking for his hand built boat, it was not until 1896 that oil was found in Corsicana as the city was trying to drill water wells, that oil had commercial value in Texas. Corsicana was the site of the first refinery in the State, built in 1897. The city was also the first in Texas to use natural gas for lighting. Until the development of the motor car, the primary use of oil was to keep down the dust on the streets.

The modern day oil industry began when the Lucas Gusher came in. That finding resulted in the formation of Texaco and Gulf oil companies, and it spurred the search for oil that was to continue in the state for decades to follow and have a profound effect on the economy and development of Texas and the nation.

The last active wooden derrick can be seen in Pioneer Park in Kermit, west of Odessa. In Kilgore is the East Texas Oil Museum on the Kilgore College campus. A tribute to the pioneers of the Texas oil industry, it houses photographs, geological tools and equipment, audiovisual presentations and a re-created 1930's boom town.

 **Bulverde**

HOMESTEAD BED & BREAKFAST

1324 Bulverde Road
Bulverde 78163
Reservations: 210 980 2571

Innkeepers:	James & Mary Jane Johnsen Owners
Open:	All Year
Facilities:	1 Bedroom-1 Bathroom Guest House
Breakfast:	Full OYO
Rates:	$75 For 2 Guests
Payment:	Check

50

Homestead Bed & Breakfast sits in the heart of a 300 acre working ranch and is part of a 12.5 acre generational trust established for the descendants of the Krause and Bremer families. Homestead sits on the original Krause-Bremer homestead founded by George Werner Krause in 1870.

In keeping with its heritage, the owners take pride in offering a glimpse into their family history. Homestead houses many of the original antique furnishings of the Krause-Bremer families. The interior features a beaded board ceiling in the kitchen and dining room, the original hardwood floor in the main bedroom and twelve foot ceilings in some areas. This accommodation is a private home reserved for only one party at a time and features two double beds, a sleeper sofa, and a private bath. A playpen and/or a roll-away bed is available upon request.

Breakfast consists of coffee, tea, juice, baked goods and breakfast fixings in the refrigerator. Snacks and beverages are provided.

Smoking is allowed outside. Children are welcome; however, there are no provisions for pets. Reservations are required. A 20% discount is given for four or more nights.

Directions: From Austin take I-35S to New Braunfels, Right on Hwy 46W, cross under 291 and turn Left on Bulverde Road (about 5 mi.) Go 3 miles to Lazy Rd. Homestead is opposite Lazy Rd. Look for a sign by the gate.

From San Antonio take 281N. Ten miles North of 1604 on 28N, Left at the flashing light (Bulverde). Go 4 mi. to Lazy Road. Sign by gate.

Member: New Braunfels Chamber of Commerce

 **Burnet**

ROCKY REST BED & BREAKFAST
404 S. Water
Burnet 78611
Reservations: 512 756 2600

Innkeeper:	Epifiania Sheppard, Resident Owner
Open:	All Year
Facilities:	3 Bedrooms, 1 Pvt Bath, 1 Shared
Breakfast:	Full
Rates:	$55 - $60 For 2 Guests
Payment:	Check

AIRY MOUNT HISTORIC INN
Rt. 3, Box 280
Burnett 78611
Reservations: 512 756 4149

Innkeeper:	Charles Hayman, Resident Owner
Open:	All Year
Facilities:	3 Bedrooms, All Private Baths
Breakfast:	Gourmet
Rates:	$75 - $100 For 2 Guests
Payment:	MC,Visa,Check

WILLIAMS POINT BED & BREAKFAST
16 Lakeside Dr
Burnett 78611
Reservations: 512 756 2074

Innkeepers:	Art & Pauline Williams, Res. Owners
Open:	All Year
Facilities:	3 Bedrooms, 2 Pvt Bath, 1 Shared
Breakfast:	Full
Rates:	$35 - $45 For 2 Guests
Payment:	Check

BURNET

Named Bluebonnet Capital of Texas by the 67th Texas Legislature, Burnet is known for its beautiful display of wild flowers each Spring. Established in 1849, the town grew around frontier Fort Croghan.

One of the most ancient geological area of the world, visitors come year round to see two miles of underground fantasy, hideout of outlaws, home of prehistoric cavemen and the site of secret gunpowder manufacture for the Confederate armies, at Longhorn Cavern about eleven miles Southwest of town via U.S. 281.

Well worth your time is Vanishing Texas River Cruise on Lake Buchanan, which operates year round. From mid November through February, the cruise visits the wintering grounds of the American Bald Eagles. Also offered is a tour of Lake Buchanan with a stop at Fall Creek Vineyards for a visit and sampling of the vineyard's award-winning wines.

The Hill Country flyer runs through Hill Country from Cedar Park City Hall near Austin to Burnet, pulled by Engine No. 786, a 75 year old steam locomotive once displayed in downtown Austin. Travelers have a two hour scenic countryside ride and a short layover in Burnet for dining and shopping, before returning.

The Highland Lakes CAF Air Museum is the headquarters for the Confederate Air Force Hill Country Squadron and features WWII fighter planes, firearms and memorabilia.

 **Burton**

KNITTEL HOMESTEAD INN

520 Main Street
Burton 77835
Reservations: 409 289 5102

Innkeepers:	Steve & Cindy Miller
	Resident Owners
Open:	All Year
Facilities:	3 Bedrooms, All Private Baths
Breakfast:	Full
Rates:	$75 - $100 For 2 Guests
Payment:	Check

Step back in time to the turn of the century when cotton was king and Victorian style was in vogue at the Historic Knittel Homestead, a 4,000 square foot Queen Anne Victorian in all its splendor, built by Herman Knittel, a Prussian immigrant and former Texas Senator.

The house boasts an Old World free standing winding staircase transported by ship from Germany in the 1880's. The home has been added to over many years and had the first indoor bathroom in Burton. During the three year restoration of the home, German and gothic script was discovered behind wallpaper in the stair turret listing the home's 1902 builders and painters.

For a restful night there are three expansive bedrooms, each overlooking historic Burton, gateway to the Bluebonnet Trails of Washington County. Complimentary beverages and homemade delectables for an afternoon or midnight snack are available. Relax on the porches and balconies with a good book, or play games in the unique upstairs turret sitting room. The house is beautifully furnished with antiques and country-style furniture. Each bedroom has its own private bath featuring claw foot tubs, fragrant soaps and bubble bath.

Monday through Saturday mornings experience a delicious all-you-can-eat country breakfast across the street at the historic Burton Cafe. Sunday morning enjoy a full breakfast in the Inn's formal dining room. Savor offerings such as fresh Burton sausage and bacon, rich buttermilk pancakes and Bananas Foster French Toast..

Smoking and pets are not allowed. Reservations are required.

Directions: Take Burton exit off Texas Hwy 290 (between Houston & Austin.)

LONG POINT INN

Rt 1, Box 86A
Burton 77835
Reservations: 409 289 3171

Innkeepers:	Bill & Jeannie Neinast
	Resident Owners
Open:	All Year
Facilities:	3 Bedrooms
	2 Private Baths, 1 Shared
Breakfast:	Gourmet
Rates:	$75 - $85 For 2 Guests
Payment:	Amex,Check

Relax in the country quiet of a luxury home that was featured as "The Prettiest Place in the Country" in <u>Farms and Ranch Living</u>. The Inn is on the highest point in Washington County with a panoramic view of Lake Somerville. The modern home is copied from old world chalets and furnished with family heirlooms and European antiques. The balcony, fretwork and window boxes with geraniums are a picture of Europe. The stair and loft railings are copies from a centuries-old house in Norway. The German crystal chandelier in the dining room, the paintings, and the paneled and boxed ceiling in the family room, continue the continental theme.

Three bedrooms, two with private baths, are available for your comfort. Sitting rooms adjoining bedrooms have hide-a-beds for family members or groups who can share baths. Children are welcome on this 175 acre ranch where the cattle are gentle enough to pet. Cribs, playpens and high chairs are available. Smoking and pets are not permitted. Reservations are required

Your hosts will join you in a big ranch-hands breakfast served in a formal setting of china and crystal under the beautiful German crystal chandelier. A typical breakfast includes a fruit compote, fruit juices, an egg dish, grits or a potato dish, locally made German pork sausage and homemade breads, jams and jellies. Snacks and drinks are complimentary.

Bill is an attorney, a retired U.S. Army colonel, a rancher and a free-lance writer, and Jeannine has a degree in homemaking and has taught school. Both your host and hostess are conversant in German.

Directions: On FM 390, 9/10 of a mile North of Long Point

 # Calvert

OUR HOUSE BED & BREAKFAST
406 E. Texas
Calvert 77837
Reservations: 409 364 2909

Innkeepers:	Don & Brenda Shafer
	Resident Owners
Open:	All Year
Facilities:	4 Bedrooms, 2 Shared Baths
Breakfast:	Full
Rates:	$65 - $75 For 2 Guests
Payment:	Check

 # Canadian

THE EMERALD HOUSE
103 North 6th Street
Canadian 79014
Reservations: 806 323 5827

Innkeepers:	Kim Harland & Russell Dake
	Resident Owners
Open:	All Year
Facilities:	4 Bedrooms, 2 Pvt Baths, 1 Share
Breakfast:	Continental Plus
Rates:	$50 - $70 For 2 Guests
Payment:	MC,Visa,Check

Canton

HEAVENLY ACRES BED & BREAKFAST
Road# 2816 - Off Hwy #198
Canton 75103
Reservations: 800 283 0341/903 887 3016

Innkeepers:	Vickie & Marshall Ragle
	Resident Owners
Open:	All Year
Facilities:	5 Cottages, All Private Baths
Breakfast:	OYO
Rates:	$85 For 2 Guests
Payment:	All Major, Check

Canyon

COUNTRY HOME BED & BREAKFAST
Rt 1, Box 447
Canyon 79015
Reservations: 800 664 7636/806 655 7636

Innkeepers:	Tammy & Dennis Brooks
	Resident Owners
Open:	All Year
Facilities:	2 Bedrooms, 1 Shared Bath
Breakfast:	Gourmet
Rates:	$55 - $85 For 2 Guests
Payment:	All Major, Check

HUDSPETH HOUSE BED & BREAKFAST INN

1905 4th Avenue
Canyon 79015
Reservations: 806 655 9800/800 655 9809

Innkeepers:	Mark & Mary Clark, Resident Owners
Open:	All Year
Facilities:	8 Bedrooms, All Private Baths
Breakfast:	Full
Rates:	$55 - $85 For 2 Guests
Payment:	All Major, Check

THE RANCH HOUSE BED & BREAKFAST

2 Mi. South Of Canyon, Rt 1, Box 436
Canyon 79015
Reservations: 806 655 0339

Innkeeper:	Janice Cluck, Resident Owner
Open:	All Year
Facilities:	3 Bedrooms, 1 Pvt Bath, 1 Shared
Breakfast:	Gourmet
Rates:	$70 - $110 For 2 Guests
Payment:	MC,Visa,Check

 # Carmine

SUGAR HILL RETREAT BED & BREAKFAST

Sugar Hill Lane, P.O. Box 9
Carmine 78932
Reservations: 409 278 3039/409 234 2055

Innkeepers:	Diana & Reuben Wunderlich, Owners
Open:	All Year
Facilities:	4 Bedrooms, 2 Shared Baths
Breakfast:	Full
Rates:	$55 - $65 For 2 Guests
Payment:	Check

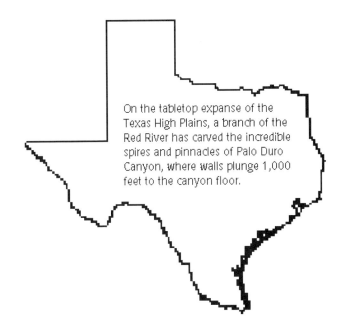

On the tabletop expanse of the Texas High Plains, a branch of the Red River has carved the incredible spires and pinnacles of Palo Duro Canyon, where walls plunge 1,000 feet to the canyon floor.

 **Castroville**

HENRI CASTRO GUESTHOUSE

1109 Fiorella Street
Castroville 78009
Reservations: 210 931 3588

Innkeeper:	Katherine Wolff
	Resident Owner
Open:	All Year
Facilities:	4 Bedrooms, 1 Private Bath
Breakfast:	Continental
Rates:	$75 For 2 Guests
Payment:	MC,Visa,Trav.Cks

The Henri Castro Guesthouse offers affordable lodging in historic surroundings. The guesthouse, hidden among beautiful trees, is located on the grounds of the Henri Castro Homestead, built 150 years ago.

Castroville was founded in 1844, when Henri Castro brought Alsatians from the French Province of Alsace and Europeans from the Rhine Valley Region to settle the rugged land west of San Antonio. The Alsatian culture and charm, a mixture of German and French heritage, is very much alive in the descendants of the early settlers who still live in the community.

Your hostess, Katherine Wolff, cordially invites you to make her guesthouse your "home-away-from-home" while enjoying this historic area.

There are sleeping accommodations for six guests. Amenities include a patio with barbecue pit, apartment sized refrigerator, full bath, microwave, and color cable TV.

A continental breakfast of juice, rolls and coffee/tea is included in the price of the lodging. There is a $10 per person charge for additional guests including children of all ages. The rate is the same during the week or on weekends. Special rates are offered to senior citizens and seven day rentals. There are a variety of fine restaurants located in Castroville. Dinner arrangements can be made for special occasions, i.e. birthdays and anniversaries. Gift certificates are also available.

No smoking or pets are allowed at the guesthouse.

Directions: From San Antonio on Hwy 90W, cross the large bridge in Castroville and turn right on Fiorella (beside Bank of America). Facility is located two blocks down the street.

 # Center Point

MARIANNE'S BED & BREAKFAST
9 Mi. East Of Kerrville
Center Point 78010
Reservations: 210 634 7489

Innkeeper:	Marianne Zuercher, Resident Owner
Open:	All Year
Facilities:	2 Bedrooms With Pvt Baths
	Plus 1 Bed-1bath Cottage
Breakfast:	Gourmet
Rates:	$60 - $80 For 2 Guests
Payment:	Check

 # Chappell Hill

MULBERRY HOUSE
Chestnut Street
Chappell Hill 77426
Reservations: 409 830 1311

Innkeepers:	Myrv & Katie Cron, Owners
Open:	All Year
Facilities:	5 Bedrooms, All Private Baths
Breakfast:	Gourmet
Rates:	$75 - $85 For 2 Guests
Payment:	Check

THE BROWNING PLANATION

Rt 1, Box 8
Chappell Hill 77426
Reservations: 409 836 6144/713 661 6761

Innkeeper:	R. P. Ganchan, Resident Owner
Open:	All Year
Facilities:	6 Bedrooms, 2 Pvt Baths,4 Shared
Breakfast:	Full
Rates:	$90 - $120 For 2 Guests
Payment:	Check

THE STAGECOACH INN

Main At Chestnut
Chappell Hill 77426
Reservations: 409 836 9515

Innkeeper:	Elizabeth Moore, Resident Owner
Open:	All Year
Facilities:	2 Bedrooms With Pvt Baths
	Two 1Bed-1bath Quarters
Breakfast:	Full
Rates:	$90 For 2 Guests
Payment:	Check

YANCH-CHRISITE HOUSE

Box 58
Chappell Hill 77426
Reservations: 713 802 1442

Innkeepers:	Ed & Carrol Chrisite, Owners
Open:	All Year
Facilities:	2 Bedroom, 2 Bath House
Breakfast:	OYO
Rates:	$65 - $95 For 2 Guests
Payment:	MC,Visa,Check

 # Clarendon

BAR H DUDE RANCH

5 Mi. NW Of Clarendon, P.O. Box 1191
Clarendon 79226
Reservations: 806 874 2634/800 627 9871

Innkeeper:	Frank Hommel, Resident Owner
Open:	All Year
Facilities:	10 Bedrooms, All Private Baths
Breakfast:	Full
Rates:	$55 - $126 For 2 Guests
Payment:	MC,Visa,Amex,Check

 # Cleburne

ANGLIN QUEEN ANNE GUEST HOUSE

723 N. Anglin St
Cleburne 76031
Reservations: 817 645 5555

Innkeepers:	Dan & Billie Ann Leach
	Resident Owners
Open:	All Year
Facilities:	5 Bedrooms, 3 Pvt Baths, 1 Shared
Breakfast:	Continental Plus
Rates:	$69 - $99 For 2 Guests
Payment:	Check

GEORGE'S CREEK INN BED & BREAKFAST
8 Mi. East Of Glen Rose
Cleburne 76031
Reservations: 817 897 2348

Innkeeper:	Kay Marcum, Resident Owner
Open:	All Year
Facilities:	4 Bedrooms, 2 Shared Baths
Breakfast:	Full
Rates:	$60 - $ 85 For 2 Guests
Payment:	Check

THE CLEBURNE HOUSE BED & BREAKFAST
201 N. Anglin Street
Cleburne 76031
Reservations: 817 641 0085

Innkeepers:	Drew & Steve Griffin
	Resident Owners
Open:	All Year
Facilities:	4 Bedrooms, 2 Pvt Baths, 1 Shared
Breakfast:	Continental Plus and Full
Rates:	$55 - $85 For 2 Guests
Payment:	Check

 # Cleveland

CHAIN-O-LAKES RESORT
BED & BREAKFAST

One Country Lane
Cleveland 77327
Reservations: 713 592 2150

Innkeeper:	James Smith, Resident Owner
Open:	All Year
Facilities:	27 Log Cabins,All Private Baths
Breakfast:	Gourmet
Rates:	$120 - $150 For 2 Guests
Payment:	All Major,Check

 # College Station

TWIN OAKS BED & BREAKFAST

3905 F & B Road
College Station 77845
Reservations: 409 846 3694

Innkeeper:	Dorothy Sens, Resident Owner
Open:	All Year
Facilities:	2 Bedrooms, All Private Baths
Breakfast:	Full
Rates:	$85 For 2 Guests
Payment:	Check

 **Columbus**

MAGNOLIA OAKS BED & BREAKFAST

634 Spring Street
Columbus 78934
Reservations: 409 732 2726

Innkeepers:	Robert & Nancy Stiles, Resident Owners
Open:	All Year
Facilities:	4 Bedrooms + Loft, All Private Baths
Breakfast:	Full
Rates:	$80 - $95 For 2 Guests
Payment:	Check

RAUMONDA BED & BREAKFAST

110 Bowie
Columbus 78934
Reservations: 409 732 2190/409 732 5135

Innkeeper:	R.F. (Buddy) Rau, Resident Owner
Open:	All Year
Facilities:	3 Bedrooms, All Private Baths
Breakfast:	Continental Plus
Rates:	$80 For 2 Guests
Payment:	Check

# Comfort

IDLEWILDE BED & BREAKFAST
115 Highway 473
Comfort 78013
Reservations: 210 995 3844

Innkeepers:	Hank Engel & Connie Cazel
	Resident Owners
Open:	All Year
Facilities:	5 Bedrooms, 3 Pvt Baths,1 Shared
Breakfast:	Full
Rates:	$77 - $93 For 2 Guests
Payment:	MC, Visa,Check

MEYER BED & BREAKFAST
845 High Street
Comfort 78013
Reservations: 210 995 2304

Innkeepers:	Joe Dobbs & Randy Nicholson
	Resident Owners
Open:	All Year
Facilities:	9 Bedrooms, All Private Baths
Breakfast:	Full
Rates:	$71 For 2 Guests
Payment:	All Major, Check

THE COMFORT COMMON

717 High Street
Comfort 78013
Reservations: 210 995 3030

Innkeepers:	Jim Lord & Boby Dent
	Resident Owners
Open:	All Year
Facilities:	7 Bedrooms, All Private Baths
Breakfast:	Full
Rates:	$55 - $95 For 2 Guests
Payment:	All Major,Check

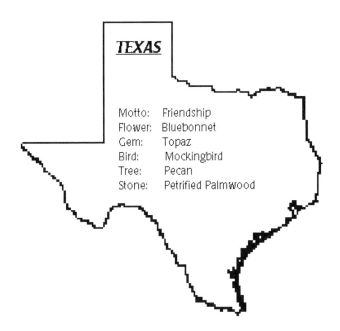

TEXAS

Motto: Friendship
Flower: Bluebonnet
Gem: Topaz
Bird: Mockingbird
Tree: Pecan
Stone: Petrified Palmwood

Conroe

BUNNY'S BED & BREAKFAST

Rt 15, Box 433D
Conroe 77304
Reservations: 409 756 4161/713 441 6895

Innkeeper:	Wanda Pavliska
	Resident Owner
Open:	All Year
Facilities:	2 Bedrooms Wtih Shared Bath
	Plus 1 Bed-1bath Cottage
Breakfast:	Full
Rates:	$60 - $80 For 2 Guests
Payment:	Check

Look for a sign mounted on an old wagon wheel saying "Bunny's Bed & Breakfast" and you'll see a two story Country Victorian house nestled on the gentle hills just outside the hustle and bustle of Conroe. It is waiting for guests to come, relax, enjoy and feel pampered. Arriving at this bed and breakfast is a treat in itself. Guests drive along a winding, tree canopied country road, past fields of contentedly grazing cows and horses and enjoy the fields of wildflowers in the Spring.

The entire home is furnished in antiques and beckons guests to rock on the front porch, take a dip in the pool (in season), or just enjoy the peaceful atmosphere.

Two spacious upstairs rooms with a comfortable sitting area share a bath. Across the back yard is a picturesque separate cottage with a private bath for those guests who like complete privacy.

A full breakfast is served in the dining room or on the front porch. Hostess Wanda Pavliska serves her guests refreshments upon their arrival and has complimentary snacks and beverages available.

Reservations are required. Senior citizen rates are offered.

Smoking is permitted outside only. Children twelve years or older are welcome. Pets are not allowed. Check out time is 11:00 a.m.

Directions: From I-45 take 285H West for 5.5 miles and go left on Leonidus Horton Road. Take first right and Bunny's is the 3rd house on the right.

Member: Conroe Chamber of Commerce

HEATHER'S GLEN ...
A BED & BREAKFAST AND MORE!

200 E. Phillips
Conroe 77301
Reservations: 713 768 8651/409 441 6611

Innkeepers:	Ed & Jamie George
	Resident Owners
Open:	All Year
Facilities:	6 Bedrooms, All Private Baths
Breakfast:	Continental Plus
	And Kitchen Privileges
Rates:	$65 - $95 For 2 Guests
Payment:	MC,Visa,Amex,Check

Heather's Glen...a Bed & Breakfast & More is a grand old two story mansion built around the turn of the century. Today this renovated structure stands as proud as the old estate, with verandas and porches reminiscent of another time. Appointed with a careful blend of antiques and decorated from the Victorian era, it accommodates the discriminating tastes of experienced travelers.

The home has twelve foot ceilings throughout and original heart of pine flooring that gleams with pride as it supports two staircases (one with electric chair glide). The interior has been restored to an authentic period look without sacrificing modern convenience. The furnishings also reflect the grace and elegance of the past visibly with lace curtains at antique glassed windows.

The unique lodging has five guest rooms from which to choose, each with its own telephone and private bath containing Ralph Lauren linens. The option of an adjoining sunroom that sleeps two is offered. Two rooms boast the luxury of double Jacuzzi's. All beds have very expensive feather down ticks and feather beds. . . what a delight to sleep in!!

A wheelchair ramp makes the downstairs accessible to the handicapped. Smoking is limited to the veranda and porches. Heather's Glen is not suitable for younger children. Pets are not allowed. Weekday rates Sunday through Thursday, except holidays.

Directions: I-45 North Exit 105, East across railroad tracks. Take left at 2nd street and you will be facing Heather's Glen.

Member: Texas Hotel & Motel Assn

Corpus Christi

BAY BREEZE BED & BREAKFAST

201 Louisianna
Corpus Christi 78404
Reservations: 512 882 4123

Innkeepers:	Perry & FrankTompkins, Res. Owners
Open:	All Year
Facilities:	4 Bedrooms, All Private Baths
Breakfast:	Full
Rates:	$57 - $85 For 2 Guests
Payment:	Check

BAY HAVEN BED & BREAKFAST

2 Blks From Water
Corpus Christi 78415
Reservations: 512 853 1222

Innkeeper:	C. J. Burgin
Open:	All Year
Facilities:	2 Bedrooms, All Private Baths
Breakfast:	Continental Plus
Rates:	$70 - $75 For 2 Guests
Payment:	Check For Deposit

CAPE COMFORT BED & BREAKFAST

4 Blks From Bay
Corpus Christi 78413
Reservations: 512 853 1222

Innkeeper:	Mrs. Rene Hausman, Resident Owner
Open:	All Year
Facilities:	2 Bedrooms, All Private Baths
Breakfast:	Continental Plus
Rates:	$54 - $60 For 2 Guests
Payment:	Check

LA MAISON DU SOLEIL

Southside Neighborhood
Corpus Christi 78415
Reservations: 512 853 1222

Innkeeper:	Peg Braswell, Resident Owner
Open:	All Year
Facilities:	1 Bedroom, Private Bath
Breakfast:	Full
Rates:	$70 - $75 For 2 Guests
Payment:	Cash Preferred

PARKVIEW BED & BREAKFAST

Southside Neighborhood
Corpus Christi 78415
Reservations: 512 853 1222

Innkeeper:	Cindy Ehrmann, Resident Owner
Open:	All Year
Facilities:	2 Bedrooms, 1 Pvt Bath, 1 Shared
Breakfast:	Continental Plus
Rates:	$54 - $60 For 2 Guests
Payment:	Check For Deposit

CONNOISSEUR OF THE COAST
BED AND BREAKFAST

710 S. Tancahua St
Corpus Christi 78401
Reservations: 512 882 2440

Innkeeper:	Linda Cottingham
	Resident Owner
Open:	All Year
Facilities:	5 Bedrooms
	2 Private Baths, 2 Shared
Breakfast:	Full & Continental
Rates:	$55 - $75 For 2 Guests
Payment:	Check

Connoisseur of the Coast bed and breakfast was given as a wedding gift in 1920 and was in the same family until your hostess, Linda Cottingham, purchased it a year ago.

The first home built on Tancahua Street (the main artery leading out from downtown), it has been renovated with central air/heat and beautiful ceiling fans in each bedroom. The rooms are comfortably furnished, and the bathrooms are tiled and spacious.

Your hostess says she uses family linens and silver "as I don't like a bed and breakfast that seems impersonal". The gardens for this bed and breakfast are like an oasis in the heart of the city. Business travelers can forget the daily hustle and bustle and unwind. Linda recently purchased the property next door, so there is now ample parking, even for RV's.

During the week a continental plus breakfast is served to guests. On the weekend a full breakfast is included.

Limited smoking on the property. Pets are not allowed. Children welcome. Guests receive 7th night stay free. Entire house can be rented (sleeps seven guests on one King, one Double, one Queen and one Twin bed) for $135. Senior citizen rates are offered. Lunch is available at additional cost by arrangement with hostess.

Swimming and exercise facilities are only two blocks away. For guests who like to get in a game of tennis or golf, there are facilities nearby. Reservations are required. Complimentary beverages offered by hostess.

Directions: Turn off Shoreline Drive at Park (look for City Coliseum at 402 S. Shoreline). Drive up bluff on Park two blocks, turn left on Tancahua to house.

PELICAN BED & BREAKFAST
Southside Neighborhood
Corpus Christi 78415
Reservations: 512 853 1222

Innkeeper:	Kay White, Resident Owner
Open:	All Year
Facilities:	2 Bedrooms, 1 Shared Bath
Breakfast:	Continental Plus
Rates:	$51-$54/Thu-Sat Only
Payment:	Check For Deposit

PRIMROSE COTTAGE BED & BREAKFAST
6 Blocks From Water
Corpus Christi 78415
Reservations: 512 853 1222

Innkeeper:	Margie Kress, Resident Owner
Open:	All Year
Facilities:	1 Bedroom, Private Bath
Breakfast:	Continental Plus
Rates:	$60 - $66 For 2 Guests
Payment:	Check For Deposit

THE SEAGULL BED & BREAKFAST
2 Blocks From Water
Corpus Christi 78415
Reservations: 512 853 1222

Innkeeper:	Evelyn Bookout, Resident Owner
Open:	All Year
Facilities:	2 Bedrooms, All Private Baths
Breakfast:	Full
Rates:	$54 - $60 For 2 Guests
Payment:	Check For Deposit

THE WHITE HOUSE BED & BREAKFAST

Southside Neighborhood
Corpus Christi 78415
Reservations: 512 853 1222

Innkeeper:	Jean White, Resident Owner
Open:	All Year
Facilities:	1 Bedroom, Private Bath
Breakfast:	Full
Rates:	$70 - $75 For 2 Guests
Payment:	Check For Deposit

THE WIMBERLY BED & BREAKFAST

Southside Neighborhood
Corpus Christi 78415
Reservations: 512 853 1222

Innkeeper:	Peggy Tweker, Resident Owner
Open:	All Year
Facilities:	3 Bedrooms, All Private Baths
Breakfast:	Full
Rates:	$87 - $90 For 2 Guests
Payment:	Check For Deposit

WOOD DUCK BED & BREAKFAST
Southside Neighborhood
Corpus Christi 78415
Reservations: 512 853 1222

Innkeeper:	Beverly Houghton, Resident Owner
Open:	All Year
Facilities:	2 Bedrooms, 1 Shared Bath
Breakfast:	Full
Rates:	$72 - $75 For 2 Guests
Payment:	Check For Deposit

 **Corsicana**

ASHMORE INN
220 North 14th Street
Corsicana 75110
Reservations: 903 872 7311

Innkeepers:	Dottie & Dwight Ashmore Resident Owners
Open:	All Year
Facilities:	4 Bedrooms, All Private Baths
Breakfast:	Gourmet
Rates:	$75 - $110 For 2 Guests
Payment:	Check

MAGNOLIA HOUSE BED & BREAKFAST

420 West 6th Avenue
Corsicana 75110
Reservations: 903 872 2577

Innkeeper:	Jeri Cargelose, Resident Owner
Open:	All Year
Facilities:	4 Bedrooms, 2 Shared Baths
Breakfast:	Full
Rates:	$65 For 2 Guests
Payment:	MC,Visa,Check

 **Crockett**

WARFIELD HOUSE BED & BREAKFAST

712 E. Houston Avenue
Crockett 75835
Reservations: 409 544 4037

Innkeepers:	Jerry & Judy Teague, Resident Owners
Open:	All Year
Facilities:	4 Bedrooms, All Private Baths
Breakfast:	Gourmet
Rates:	$75 - $100 For 2 Guests
Payment:	MC,Visa,Amex,Check

LOG CABIN BED & BREAKFAST

Route 4, Box 106 K
Crockett 75835
Reservations: 409 636 2002/800 723 4829

Innkeeper:	Greta Hicks, Resident Owner
Open:	All Year
Facilities:	3 Bedrooms
	1 Private Bath, 1 Shared
Breakfast:	Full Or Continental Plus
Rates:	$95 - $125 For 2 Guests
Payment:	MC,Visa,Check

Log Cabin Bed & Breakfast is longhorn cows, fishing ponds, wildlife, birds, hiking trails and forty acres of secluded, relaxed, romantic, rural quietness located on the fringe of the East Texas Pineywoods.

The native log interior is enhanced by the lodge style furnishings and the massive native stone fireplace. Lodge pole pine beds and antiques compliment the modern log home which is packed with American Indian, primitive and cowboy accent pieces. The library includes a collection of the classics, poetry, and inspirational materials and resource books on Texas wildflowers, birds and history.

Log Cabin Bed & Breakfast is a place to sit on the front porch and watch the grass grow, to lounge in the hammock in the cool shade, enjoy the hot tub, or a place to do just nothing at all . . . .

Guests have the option of a Continental Plus or Full breakfast, either enjoying each other's company at the massive oak dining table, taking a tray to the porch, or eating on the deck under the shade of the red bud tree. Your hostess, Greta Hicks, offers complimentary snacks and beverages. Lunch and/or dinner is available at additional cost.

Pets are not allowed. Smoking is limited to the deck and porch. Reservations are required. Ask about off season rates. Discounts are offered for more than a three night stay, for groups and for renting the entire facility.

Directions: Ten miles South of Crockett, off FM 2110. Specifics released upon confirmation.

Member: Texas Hotel & Motel Assoc.

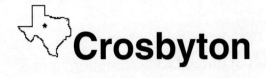 **Crosbyton**

SMITH HOUSE BED & BREAKFAST
306 W. Aspen
Crosbyton 79322
Reservations: 806 675 2178/800 749 3178

Innkeepers:	Terry & Sandy Cash, Resident Owners
Open:	All Year
Facilities:	10 Bedrooms, 6 Pvt Baths,4 Shared
Breakfast:	Gourmet
Rates:	$50 - $85 For 2 Guests
Payment:	MC, Visa,Check

 **Daingerfield**

MABERRY COTTAGE BED & BREAKFAST
1403 Maberry Road
Daingerfield 75638
Reservations: 903 645 3227

Innkeepers:	Marvin & Linda Maberry
	Resident Owenrs
Open:	All Year
Facilities:	2 Bedroom, 1 Bath Cottage
Breakfast:	Continental Plus
Rates:	$55 -100 For 2 Guests
Payment:	Check

 **Dallas**

BETTY & GEORGE'S BED & BREAKFAST

15869 Nedra Way
Dallas 75248
Reservations: 214 386 4323

Innkeepers:	Betty & George Hyde, Resident Owners
Open:	All Year
Facilities:	2 Bedrooms, Pvt Bath
Breakfast:	Full
Rates:	$45 - $50 For 2 Guests
Payment:	Check

THE AMERICAN DREAM BED & BREAKFAST

P.O. Box 670275 (Call for Directions)
Dallas 75367
Reservations: 214 357 6536/800 373 2690

Innkeepers:	Patricia & Andrew, Resident Owners
Open:	All Year
Facilities:	2 Bedrooms, Pvt Bath
Breakfast:	Continental Plus
Rates:	$69 for 2 Guests
Payment:	MC,Visa,Check

INN ON FAIRMOUNT

3701 Fairmount St
Dallas 75219
Reservations: 214 522 2800 Fax: 214 522 2898

Innkeeper:	Michael McVay, Resident Owner
Open:	All Year
Facilities:	7 Bedrooms, All Private Baths
Breakfast:	Continental
Rates:	$80 - $120 For 2 Guests
Payment:	MC, Visa,Check

The Inn on Fairmount, a Bed and Breakfast Inn, is located in the heart of the Oak Lawn -Turtle Creek area, just minutes from dozens of fine restaurants and clubs, less than two minutes from the Dallas Market Center and just ten minutes from the Arts District of Dallas for those who enjoy the ambiance of an inn and the luxury of a fine hotel.

Double bedrooms have Queen size beds with private bath . . .Twin bedrooms have twin beds with private bath . . .Mini-Suites have a King size bed and Queen size sofa bed with private baths . . .Suites have King size beds, sitting room with Queen size sofa bed and private bath.

Amenities include direct dial telephones and remote control color televisions. A beautifully decorated Lounge is available for the use of the Inn's guests, and there is a deck with Jacuzzi.

Each morning, just outside your door, you will find freshly brewed coffee along with a morning paper. Enjoy these while dressing and then join other guests in the Lounge for a complimentary continental breakfast of fruit juices, seasonal fruit and assorted pastries with butter and jam. Each evening your host, Michael McVay, invites guests to the Lounge for wine and cheese.

Smoking is limited. Children 14 and older are welcome. No pets are allowed. Reservations are required. Rates are based on single or double occupancy and there is a $10 charge for each additional person per night. Discounts for extended stay upon request.

Directions: ½ Mile East of I-35E at Oaklawn Avenue exit.

 **Denison**

IVY BLUE BED & BREAKFAST
1100 West Sears
Denison 75020
Reservations: 903 463 2479

Innkeepers:	Lane & Tammy Segerstrom
	Resident Owners
Open:	All Year
Facilities:	6 Bedrooms, 3 Pvt Baths, 2 Shared
Breakfast:	Gourmet
Rates:	$65 - $145 For 2 Guests
Payment:	MC,Visa,Check

THE MOLLY CHERRY BED & BREAKFAST
200 West Prospect
Denison 75020
Reservations: 903 465 0575

Innkeepers:	Jim & Regina Widener
	Resident Owners
Open:	All Year
Facilities:	Inquire
Breakfast:	Full
Rates:	Check Innkeeper
Payment:	Inquire

 **Denton**

THE REDBUD INN
815 North Locust
Denton 76201
Reservations: 817 565 6414

Innkeepers:	John & Donna Morris, Resident Owners
Open:	All Year
Facilities:	5 Bedrooms, All Private Baths
Breakfast:	Full
Rates:	$49 - $75 For 2 Guests
Payment:	All Major, Check

 **Dickinson**

THE DESEL HOUSE - CIRCA 1895
5303 Desel Dr
Dickinson 77539
Reservations: 713 337 1397

Innkeeper:	Terry Brass-Nash, Resident Owner
Open:	All Year
Facilities:	Two 1 Bed-1 Bath Suites
Breakfast:	Continental Plus
Rates:	$85 - $135 For 2 Guests
Payment:	All Major, Check

Dripping Springs

COUNTRY AIR GUEST HOUSE

HC 01, Box 76C
Dripping Springs 78620
Reservations: 512 858 4535

Innkeepers:	Janet & Wayman Curry
	Resident Owners
Open:	All Year
Facilities:	2 Bedroom, 1 Bath Guest House
Breakfast:	Continental OYO
Rates:	$80 For 2 Guests
Payment:	Check

Country Air Guest House, affectionately called "The Little White House" by the locals, was constructed in the early 20's by the Hilgar Haywood family. In 1928 it was purchased by the newly married Dr. Leonard and Faye Twidwell who remodeled it to include plumbing and enclosed kitchen cabinets, one of the first homes in the area to boast these modern conveniences! It served as both their primary and secondary residence until it was purchased by your hosts in 1980.

The house is furnished with a blend of antique and country furniture. Tastefully decorated in a very unique aviation theme which is carried throughout in a most interesting manner. The guest house even has a screened back porch overlooking Caddell Creek (for those guests who wish to grab a pole and try their luck with the lunker bass waiting there).

The guest house sleeps four persons. The master bedroom has a Queen size bed and the second bedroom a double bed. The bath has a tub/shower combination and the kitchen is fully equipped including a microwave.

Breakfast consists of coffee, tea, juice, milk, cereal, fresh fruits in season, and muffins to enjoy at your leisure. Pets are allowed by special permission. Smoking is not allowed. There are no provisions for children. Reservations are required. Rates are for double occupancy. Check in time is 3 p.m. and check out is at 12 noon. First night advance deposit required, balance on arrival.

Directions: Go nine miles West of Dripping Springs on 290 to Henly. Turn on RR165 to Blanco. B&B is two miles down Ranch Road 165 (look for signs on left).

Member: Texas Hotel & Motel Assoc.

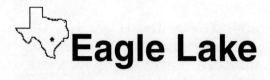# Eagle Lake

EAGLE HILL INN & RETREAT
307 E. State Street
Eagle Lake 77434
Reservations: 800 324 3551

Innkeeper:	Linda Ferugson, Manager
Open:	All Year
Facilities:	10 Bedrooms, 4 Pvt Baths,6 Shared
Breakfast:	Full
Rates:	$85 - $150 For 2 Guests
Payment:	MC,Visa,Amex,Check

# Eddy

BELLE PLAIN BED & BREAKFAST
Box 249
Eddy 76524
Reservations: 817 859 5805

Innkeeper:	Foy DuBois, Resident Owner
Open:	All Year
Facilities:	2 Bedrooms, Shared Bath
Breakfast:	Full
Rates:	$75 - $85 For 2 Guests
Payment:	Check

THE FLOWERS HOUSE
600 West 3rd
Eddy 76524
Reservations: 817 859 5510

Innkeepers:	Jim & Dianne Payne, Resident Owners
Open:	All Year
Facilities:	3 Bedrooms, All Private Baths
Breakfast:	Full
Rates:	$65 - $75 For 2 Guests
Payment:	Check

Edgewood

CROOKED CREEK FARM BED & BREAKFAST
CR 310, Hwy 19
Edgewood 75117
Reservations: 903 896 1284/800 766 0790

Innkeeper:	Dorthy Thornton, Resident Owner
Open:	All Year
Facilities:	5 Bedrooms, 2 Pvt Baths, S Shared
Breakfast:	Full
Rates:	$65 - $80 For 2 Guests
Payment:	Check

 **El Paso**

BERGMANN INN
10009 Trinidad Drive
El Paso 79925
Reservations: 915 599 1398

Innkeeper:	David Bergman, Resident Owner
Open:	All Year
Facilities:	2 Bedrooms, Shared Bath
Breakfast:	Continental Plus
Rates:	$50 For 2 Guests
Payment:	Check

SUNSET HEIGHTS BED & BREAKFAST INN
717 W. Yandell Ave
El Paso 79902
Reservations: 915 544 1743/800 767 8513

Innkeepers:	R. Barnett & Ms. R. Martinez,MD
	Resident Owners
Open:	All Year
Facilities:	5 Bedrooms, All Private Baths
Breakfast:	Gourmet
Rates:	$80 - $145 For 2 Guests
Payment:	All Major, Check

 **Elgin**

BRINKLEY'S BED & BREAKFAST
1212 North Main
Elgin 78621
Reservations: 512 281 4375/800 231 5426

Innkeepers:	Rosiland & Gary Brinkley
	Resident Owners
Open:	All Year
Facilities:	2 Bedroom With Pvt Bath
	Plus 1 Bed-1 Bath Bungalow
Breakfast:	Full
Rates:	$50 For 2 Guests
Payment:	Check

NANA'S BED & BREAKFAST
3 Mi. From Town On FM 3000
Elgin 78621
Reservations: 512 281 3243

Innkeepers:	Joanna & Kay Hicks, Resident Owners
Open:	All Year
Facilities:	1 Bedroom, 1 Bath Suite
Breakfast:	Full
Rates:	$55 For 2 Guests
Payment:	Check

Eliasville

(In Young County - So. of Wichita Falls)

ANDREWS HOUSE BED & BREAKFAST
102 Park Street
Eliasville 76438
Reservations: 817 362 4243

Innkeepers:	Mike & Melba Riggs, Resident Owners
Open:	All Year
Facilities:	2 Bedrooms, 1 Bath
Breakfast:	OYO
Rates:	$40 - 69 For 2 Guests
Payment:	Diners Club,Check

Emory

SWEET SEASONS BED & BREAKFAST
630 Honeysuckle Lane
Emory 75440
Reservations: 903 473 3706

Innkeepers:	Brad & Susie Joiner, Resident Owners
Open:	All Year
Facilities:	3 Bedrooms, 2 Baths In 2 Cottages
Breakfast:	Full
Rates:	$79 - $89 For 2 Guests
Payment:	MC,Visa,Check

MARSHALL

Settled in 1839, Marshall is the seat of Harrison County. When Texas seceded from the Union in 1861, this city was one of the biggest and wealthiest in the State, producing powder and ammunition for the Confederacy, saddles, harnesses and clothing.

Centered around the 1896 Ginocchio Hotel in the heart of downtown Marshall, the Ginocchio National Historic District is one of the state's finest examples of Victorian architecture.

The Harrison County Historical Society Museum in the remodeled former county courthouse, exhibits Caddo Indian artifacts, pioneer and Civil War displays, Lady Bird Johnson memorabilia and the Y. A. Tittle display. Visitors are attracted to the Star Family State Historic Site, better known as Maplecroft, which was constructed of materials shipped from New Orleans and reflects the Italianate style then popular.

The nearby lush, primeval Caddo Lake area is just a short drive to Karnack. While there, travelers may visit the birthplace of Mrs. Lyndon B. Johnson which is constructed of bricks made by slaves and built before the Civil War. The structure is now open to the public. Caddo Lake State Park (480 acres beside Caddo Lake) is an area once occupied by the Caddo Indians, a tribe quite advanced in civilization, where fishing, swimming, boating, hiking and nature trails, among other attractions, are available to visitors.

Marshall Pottery, established in 1896, is one of the largest manufacturers of glazed pottery in the U.S. Demonstrations of pottery making and firing are held on a regular basis.

 **Ennis**

Raphael House

500 W. Ennis Ave
Ennis 75119
Reservations: 214 875 1555

Innkeepers:	Brian & Dana Cody Wolf
	Resident Owners
Open:	All Year
Facilities:	6 Bedrooms, All Private Baths
Breakfast:	Full on Weekend
	and Continental Plus Mid Week
Rates:	$52 - $100 For 2 Guests
Payment:	All Major,Check

Located in the heart of a National Register Historic District, this 16 room mansion was built in 1906 in the Neoclassic Revival style. Architecturally unchanged in the 1988 restoration, Raphael House still contains much of the original furnishings, museum quality antiques, rich wall coverings and luxurious fabrics. Texas Highways calls it "a decorators dream" with its twelve foot ceilings and extensive woodwork.

Amenities include down comforters/pillows, claw foot tubs, English toiletries, telephones and turn down service. Guests also have membership privileges at a private tennis and health club with indoor/outdoor courts, pool, weight room and spa. Also available on site is in-room Swedish massage, a swimming pool and hot tub/sauna.

The six guestrooms are perfect for honeymoon, anniversary or weekend getaway. Each bedroom is uniquely decorated and has a private bath. Upon arrival, guests may choose any available room.

Continental Plus breakfast is served to guests during the week and a full breakfast, afternoon tea and snacks/drinks are served on weekends.

Hosts Brian and Danna feel that Raphael House has all the ingredients to make a splendid holiday or an enjoyable business stay, and say "For you our commitment is always the same - to provide the very best."

Smoking is not permitted and pets are not allowed. Children accepted at hosts' discretion. Reservations recommended. Ask about mid week corporate single's rates.

Directions: From I-45 take Exit #251, go West exactly one mile. From I-35 exit Hwy 287, go East 18 miles.

Member: Historic Hotel Assn of Texas, National Trust for Historic Preservation

 **Fayetteville**

COUNTRY AT HEART BED & BREAKFAST GUEST COTTAGE
105 N. Rusk
Fayetteville 78940
Reservations: 409 378 2718

Innkeepers:	Shirley & Rick Sodek, Resident Owners
Open:	All Year
Facilities:	1 Bedroom With Bath
Breakfast:	Continental Plus
Rates:	$60 - $75 For 2 Guests
Payment:	Check

LIVE OAK STREET GUEST COTTAGE
206 N. Live Oak
Fayetteville 78940
Reservations: 409 968 8787

Innkeeper:	Lucille Rippel, Owner
Open:	All Year
Facilities:	1 Bedroom Cottage With Bath
Breakfast:	OYO
Rates:	$65 For 2 Guests
Payment:	Check

SCATTERED OAKS COTTAGE
Fm 1291
Fayetteville 78940
Reservations: 409 378 2236

Innkeeper:	Emilie Bertsch, Owner
Open:	All Year
Facilities:	2 Bedrooms, Shared Bath
Breakfast:	OYO
Rates:	Call For Rates
Payment:	Check

THE COTTAGE

Market Street
Fayetteville 78940
Reservations: 800 256 7721/409 378 4218

Innkeepers:	Hal & Dorothy Stall, Owners
Open:	All Year
Facilities:	1 Bedroom With Bath
Breakfast:	OYO
Rates:	$65 For 2 Guests
Payment:	Check

THE FAYETTE HOUSE

Fayette Street, Off Square
Fayetteville 78940
Reservations: 800 256 7721/713 333 2260

Innkeepers:	Hal & Dorothy Stall, Owners
Open:	All Year
Facilities:	3 Bedroom Cottage With Bath
Breakfast:	OYO
Rates:	$95 For 2 Guests
Payment:	Check

Fink

GEORGETOWN HOUSE

Rt. 2, Box 240H
Fink 75076
Reservations: 903 786 6104

Innkeepers:	Ron & Linda Ivey, Managers
Open:	All Year
Facilities:	2 Bedrooms, 1 Shared Bath
Breakfast:	Continental
Rates:	$100 For 2 Guests
Payment:	All Major,Check

 **Fischer**

HARAMBE OAKS RANCH
1.5 Mi. South Of Town
Fischer 78623
Reservations: 210 935 2557

Innkeepers:	Judy Rinker & Phyllis Bigby
	Resident Owners
Open:	All Year
Facilities:	24 Bedrooms, All Pvt Baths
Breakfast:	Full
Rates:	$85 - $110 For 2 Guests
Payment:	Check

 **Floydada**

HISTORIC LAMPLIGHTER INN
102 South 5th
Floydada 79235
Reservations: 806 983 3035

Innkeepers:	Evelyn Branch & Roxanna Cummings
	Resident Owners
Open:	All Year
Facilities:	20 Bedrooms, 7 Pvt Baths, 3 Shared
Breakfast:	Full
Rates:	$40 - $50 For 2 Guests
Payment:	Check

 **Fort Davis**

BOYNTON HOME GUEST LODGE
#5 Delores Mountain
Fort Davis 79734
Reservations: 915 426 3123/800 359 5020

Innkeeper:	E.J. Boynton, Resident Owner
Open:	All Year
Facilities:	5 Bedrooms, All Private Baths
Breakfast:	Full
Rates:	$55 - $75 For 2 Guests
Payment:	MC,Visa,Check

NEILL MUSEUM BED & BREAKFAST INN
7 Blocks West Of Courthouse
Fort Davis 79734
Reservations: 915 426 3838/426 3969

Innkeeper:	Shirley Vickers, Resident Owner
Open:	All Year
Facilities:	2 Bedrooms, Shared Bath
Breakfast:	Continental
Rates:	$65 For 2 Guests
Payment:	Check

WAYSIDE INN BED & BREAKFAST
400 W. 4th St
Fort Davis 79734
Reservations: 915 426 3535/800 582 7510

Innkeepers:	J.W. & Anna Beth Ward Resident Owners
Open:	All Year
Facilities:	7 Bedrooms, All Private Baths
Breakfast:	Full
Rates:	$60 For 2 Guests
Payment:	All Major, Check

The Veranda Country Inn
Bed & Breakfast

210 Court Avenue
Fort Davis 79734
Reservations: 915 426 2233

Innkeepers:	Paul & Kathie Woods
	Resident Owners
Open:	All Year
Facilities:	8 Bedrooms, All Private Baths
Breakfast:	Full
Rates:	$59 - $74 For 2 Guests
Payment:	MC,Visa, Disc,Check

Located in Fort. Davis, The Veranda is a spacious historic inn built in 1883. This unique adobe building, has two foot thick walls and twelve foot ceilings, and is furnished with antiques and collectibles. Its walled gardens and quiet courtyards provide weary professionals and exploring travelers a change of pace and lifestyle in the year-round dry and mild climate of mile-high Fort Davis.

The Veranda has two types of accommodations: large, single rooms and even larger, two-room suites. Two of these contain two double beds each. The other six each have one King size bed. All rooms and suites have a private bath. Among the delights at this bed and breakfast are mahogany furnishings, arched beveled mirrors, walnut paneling, and a natural quartz, crystalline fireplace. Your hosts, Paul and Kathie Woods, also provide guests with thick, Egyptian cotton velour robes.

Breakfast is served from 7-9 a.m. Diners may choose from a collection of goodies including Kathie's special breakfast soufflé, German farmer's omelet, ham, smoked sausage, bacon, homemade biscuits, muffins and coffee cake. A lighter breakfast of fresh fruit, yogurt, dry cereal and hot cereal is also available.

This is a tobacco-free facility including all rooms, porches and grounds. Reservations are required. Discounts for extended stays. Check in is at 3 p.m. and check out is 11 a.m.

Directions: 45 minutes South of IH10 in Ft. Davis, one block West of Ft. Davis Courthouse.

Member: Professional Assn of Innkeepers Int'l, Texas Hotel/Motel Assn, Hist. Hotel Assn of Texas

Fort Worth

AZALEA PLANTATION
1400 Robinwood Drive
Fort Worth 76111
Reservations: 817 838 5882

Innkeepers:	Martha & Richard Linnartz, Owners
Open:	All Year
Facilities:	4 Bedrooms, All Private Baths
Breakfast:	Full
Rates:	$89 - $120 For 2 Guests
Payment:	MC,Visa,Disc,Check

MISS MOLLY'S HOTEL BED & BREAKFAST
109-1/2 W. Exchange
Fort Worth 76106
Reservations: 817 626 1522/800 99-Molly

Innkeeper:	Mark Hancock, Resident Owner
Open:	All Year
Facilities:	8 Bedrooms, 1 Pvt Bath, 3 Shared
Breakfast:	Continental Plus
Rates:	$85 - $150 For 2 Guests
Payment:	All Major,Check

OAKLAND INN BED & BREAKFAST
2409 Oakland Blvd.
Fort Worth 76111
Reservations: 817 534 2026

Innkeeper:	Ruth McKinley, Resident Owner
Open:	All Year
Facilities:	4 Bedrooms, 2 Shared Baths
Breakfast:	Continental
Rates:	$50 For 2 Guests
Payment:	Check

THE COLONY BED & BREAKFAST

2611 Glendale Ave
Fort Worth 76106
Reservations: 817 624 1981

Innkeepers:	Gloria & Robert Sample
	Resident Owners
Open:	All Year
Facilities:	3 Bedrooms, 1 Shared Bath
Breakfast:	Full
Rates:	$65 For 2 Guests
Payment:	Check

THE TEXAS WHITE HOUSE

1417 Eighth Ave
Fort Worth 76104
Reservations: 817 923 3597

Innkeepers:	James Sexton & Grover McMains
Open:	All Year
Facilities:	3 Bedrooms, All Private Baths
Breakfast:	Gourmet
Rates:	$85 - $95 For 2 Guests
Payment:	MC,Visa,Amex,Check

 **Franklin**

DREAM CATCHER GUEST RANCH

25 Mi. E. Of Franklin
Franklin 77856
Reservations: 409 279 2050

Innkeeper:	Vicky Corrington, Resident Owner
Open:	All Year
Facilities:	3 Bedrooms, 1 Shared Bath
Breakfast:	Continental Plus
Rates:	$60 - $80 For 2 Guests
Payment:	Check

Fredericksburg

A Little Waltz B&B

509 N. Cherry
Fredericksburg 78624
Reservations: 210 997 2407/210 997 5612

Innkeeper:	Anne Weigers, Resident Owner
Open:	All Year
Facilities:	1 Bedroom With Bath
Breakfast:	Gourmet
Rates:	$125 For 2 Guests
Payment:	All Major,Check

Pamper yourself at A Little Waltz. . . .secluded in your hostess' home. At this traditional bed and breakfast you will enjoy total privacy with your own entrance through antique Mexican doors, through an ivy hung patio, into your room through French doors.

The bedroom is an elegant, romantic room with an open fireplace, gorgeous antique armoire that shelters your TV, a fabulous Homestead four poster bed (and Homestead fabrics throughout), antiques and angels.

Your wonderful bathroom features a tub-for-two with a skylight for gazing at the clouds, stars and/or moon. A mural surrounds you and is reflected in the huge antique mirror.

In the morning you are treated to a gourmet feast served on family antique china in the home's marvelous dining room with its country view over open fields (decorated with a pinto pony!).

An adult accommodation for two. Children, pets and smoking are not allowed. Reservations are required. Your hostess, Anne Weigers, serves complimentary wine to those guests celebrating an anniversary, birthday, or who are on their honeymoon.

Directions: Three blocks North of Main Street Fredericksburg.

BARON'S CREEK COTTAGE

509 W. Ufer
Fredericksburg 78624
Reservations: 210 997 6578

Innkeepers:	Robert & Brenda Deming
	Resident Owners
Open:	All Year
Facilities:	1 Bedroom - 1 Bath Cottage
Breakfast:	Continental Plus
Rates:	$65 - $75 For 2 Guests
Payment:	MC,Visa,Check

Guests have called Baron's Creek Cottage a "doll house". The cottage, next to an old windmill complete with water tank, was built in 1933 by a widow. Even though it is quite small, six children were raised in this house between 1947 and 1972.

The cottage is both private and peaceful. The back deck looks out over a large back yard with trees and grass sloping to Baron's Creek. Guests like to listen to the creek as it babbles along and watch the lights reflect from it . . .the adventuresome even like to wade a bit. Taking a walk to downtown Fredericksburg is like taking a "walk in history" as guests will pass by many historic homes along the way.

For those in the romantic mood, hosts Robert and Brenda Deming, provide a CD player with a selection of music. They also provide anniversary couples with a bottle of champagne. Cable TV is provided for those who do not choose to miss that special ball game.

The cottage, furnished with antiques which lend a romantic atmosphere, consists of a living room, kitchen/dining room, bedroom and bath. A Continental Plus breakfast is included in the rate. Complimentary snacks and beverages are provided by your hosts.

Smoking is allowed outdoors. Children and pets are welcomed. Reservations are not required. Inquire about weekday off season rates.

Directions: West Main Street to S. Bowie, turn left (South) to Peach, Left on Peach, Right on Rose - Rose dead ends at cottage.

ALLEGANI'S LITTLE HORSE INN

307 S. Creek
Fredericksburg 78624
Reservations: 210 997 7448

Innkeeper:	Jani Schofield, Owner
Open:	All Year
Facilities:	2 Bedroom, 1 Bath House
Breakfast:	Continental Plus
Rates:	$85 For 2 Guests
Payment:	Check

ALLEGANI'S SUNDAY HOUSE BED & BREAKFAST

418 W. Creek St
Fredericksburg 78624
Reservations: 210 997 7448

Innkeeper:	Jani Schofield, Resident Owner
Open:	All Year
Facilities:	2 Bedroom, 1 Bath Cottage
Breakfast:	Continental Plus
Rates:	$65 For 2 Guests
Payment:	Check

ALMOST HOME BED & BREAKFAST

Enchanted Rock Highway
Fredericksburg 78624
Reservations: 210 997 8948

Innkeepers:	Sue & Rodney Seay, Managers
Open:	All Year
Facilities:	4 Bedrooms, 2 Pvt Baths, 1 Shared
Breakfast:	Continental
Rates:	$55 - $85 For 2 Guests
Payment:	Check

BIRD SONG BED & BREAKFAST

1203 N. Adams
Fredericksburg 78624
Reservations: 210 997 0111

Innkeeper:	Dy Thompson, Resident Owner
Open:	All Year
Facilities:	1 Suite With Private Bath
Breakfast:	Continental Plus
Rates:	$65 For 2 Guests
Payment:	Check

COLEMAN'S COUNTRY PLACE

HC 13, Box 52A
Fredericksburg 78624
Reservations: 210 997 9608

Innkeepers:	Donne & Gary Coleman
	Resident Owners
Open:	All Year
Facilities:	2 Bedrooms, 1 Shared Bath
Breakfast:	OYO
Rates:	$65 - $120 For 2 Guests
Payment:	Check

COUNTRY GETAWAY

Rt. 3, Box 387
Fredericksburg 78624
Reservations: 210 997 9518

Innkeepers:	Larry & Annette Casbeer
Open:	All Year
Facilities:	1 Bedroom Cottage With Bath
Breakfast:	Continental Plus
Rates:	$50 - $60 For 2 Guests
Payment:	Check

CAIN CITY COTTAGE

RR #3, Box 363
Fredericksburg 78624
Reservations: 210 997 6747

Innkeepers:	Fran & Harvey Fehrenbach
	Resident Owners
Open:	All Year
Facilities:	2 Bedroom
	1 Bath Sunday House
Breakfast:	Gourmet
Rates:	$86.20 For 2 Guests
Payment:	Check

High on a ridge overlooking the historic town of Fredericksburg, Cain City Cottage offers guests a quiet, private atmosphere with a panoramic view. You can sit on the wonderful front porch of this turn-of-the-century Sunday House and think about nothing at all and watch the grass grow.

The three room house consists of a sitting/bedroom with Queen size bed and fireplace, a kitchenette with dining space, full bath and an upstairs bedroom with twin four poster beds.

A gourmet breakfast is offered by hosts Fran & Harvey Fehrenbach.

Smoking is permitted. Children and pets are welcome. Inquire about off season rates. Discounts are given for second night and longer stays. Special occasion cakes are available with advance notice. Complimentary snacks and beverages are provided. Guests may arrange lunch in advance.

Directions: Hwy 290E from Austin. Turn Left at KOA Campground and drive one and nine tenths miles. Turn Right onto Cain city Road and go one and four tenths miles. Turn Left on Broadway and go seven tenth miles and turn into the gate with the vultures.

Member: Fredericksburg Chamber of Commerce

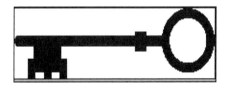

CARRIAGE HOUSE

610 Tivydale Road
Fredericksburg 78624
Reservations: 210 997 3867

Innkeepers:	Darrell & Betty Vanderford
	Resident Owners
Open:	All Year
Facilities:	2 Bedrooms, 3 Private Baths
Breakfast:	Full
Rates:	$65 For 2 Guests
Payment:	Check

Carriage House, a bed and breakfast with country elegance, was built in 1854 by German immigrants out of local limestone.

The original part of the house had only two rooms with a dog trot in the middle. Legend states the owners would tie the horses in the dog trot at night to keep the Indians from stealing them. Legend also has it that runaway slaves were hidden in the loft of the house during the Civil War.

In the early 1930's the house became The Live Oak Dairy with 30 milk cows. The dairy sold butter, cream and milk.

A beautiful sunrise or sunset can be seen from the porches, or a walk down the country road will please those guests who enjoy nature, wildflowers, birds and "quiet".

Guests will wake up to a hot cup of coffee or tea which they can enjoy on the front porch. Breakfast consists of home made biscuits, bacon and fresh eggs, gravy or grits, home made jellies and juice or seasonal Fredericksburg fruit.

Smoking is not allowed at Carriage House. Children are welcome. There are no accommodations for pets. Future plans are made for the handicapped. Reservations are required. There are nearby tennis and golf facilities.

Directions: Highway 16 South from Fredericksburg for two miles. Turn right on Tivydale Road (to airport) and go one mile. Look for the stone house on the right hand side.

COUNTRY COTTAGE INN
- NIMITZ BIRTHPLACE

249 E. Main
Fredericksburg 78624
Reservations: 214 373 9788/210 997 8549

Innkeeper:	Mrs. Jeffery Ann Webb
	Manager
Open:	All Year
Facilities:	11 Bedrooms, All Private Baths
Breakfast:	Full OYO
Rates:	$80 - $120 For 2 Guests
Payment:	MC,Visa,Check

The Country Cottage Inn - Nimitz Birthplace is made up of mellow limestone homes and courtyards. The inn is located in the direct center of Fredericksburg's historic district, yet is a country-like oasis of quiet, beauty and solitude.

One of America's greatest naval heroes, Fleet Admiral Chester W. Nimitz, was born in 1885 in one of this Inn's historic homes. The oldest two story stone house in Fredericksburg (Circa 1880) is another charming part of the inn. The architecture of graceful German homes with long porches and flourishes of gingerbread are present throughout.

Peaceful seclusion, lingering moments beneath the comforter on a soft, luxurious bed, a cozy flickering fireplace, the candlelit atmosphere of a large bubbling Jacuzzi tub for two and much more for you to discover at Country Cottage Inn.

A secluded courtyard with limestone walkways, a handcut fountain with surrounding herb garden and relaxing porch swings all add to the wonderful charm of this bed and breakfast.

There are five two-room suites, four junior suites and two double rooms that can sleep up to thirty-two plus. Eight have fireplaces, nine have Jacuzzis for two and all have private baths and entrances. You will find comfortable antique furnishings, rocking chairs, Laura Ashley linens, TV's, phones, microwaves, ceiling fans and pitchers of ice water .

Your breakfast fare may include a Southwestern egg dish, smoked peppered tenderloin, and Fredericksburg cinnamon rolls. Afternoon tea is served.

Smoking is limited. Children are welcome. Please do not bring pets. Reservations are necessary.

Member: Historic Hotel Assn of Texas

DER WEIRESHAUSEN HAUS
704 W. Travis
Fredericksburg 78624
Reservations: 210 997 7080

Innkeeper:	Shirlee Thompson, Resident Owner
Open:	All Year
Facilities:	2 Bedrooms, 1 Shared Bath
Breakfast:	Continental
Rates:	$75 - $85 For 2 Guests
Payment:	Check

EAST OF THE SUN - WEST OF THE MOON
512 W. Austin
Fredericksburg 78624
Reservations: 210 997 4981

Innkeeper:	Teresa Ray, Resident Owner
Open:	All Year
Facilities:	2 Bedrooms, 1 Shared Bath
Breakfast:	Full
Rates:	$80 - $110 For 2 Guests
Payment:	MC,Visa,Check

ENCHANTED ACRES BED & BREAKFAST
Highway 965, Upper Crabapple Rd
Fredericksburg 78624
Reservations: 210 997 7967

Innkeepers:	Rick & Laura Wilson, Resident Owners
Open:	All Year
Facilities:	1 Bedroom, Private Bath
Breakfast:	Continental Plus
Rates:	$75 - $90 For 2 Guests
Payment:	All Major, Check

FLAGG CREEK BED & BREAKFAST
Ranch Road 2093
Fredericksburg 78624
Reservations: 210 997 5363

Innkeepers:	Kathy & Ted Masser, Resident Owners
Open:	All Year
Facilities:	2 Bedrooms, 1 Shared Bath
Breakfast:	Continental
Rates:	$90 For 2 Guests
Payment:	Check

INN AT THE END OF THE LANE
P.O. Box 469
Fredericksburg 78624
Reservations: 210 997 0168

Innkeepers:	Russ & Myretta Weaver Resident Owners
Open:	All Year
Facilities:	2 Bedrooms, 1 Shared Bath
Breakfast:	Full
Rates:	$79.50 For 2 Guests
Payment:	MC,Check

INN ON THE CREEK BED & BREAKFAST
107 N. Washington
Fredericksburg 78624
Reservations: 210 997 9585

Innkeeper:	Diane Hauerland, Resident Owner
Open:	All Year
Facilities:	6 Bedrooms, All Private Baths
Breakfast:	Full
Rates:	$85 - $110 For 2 Guests
Payment:	MC,Visa,Check

MAGNOLIA HOUSE

101 E Hackberry
Fredericksburg 78624
Reservations: 210 997 0306/800 880 4374

Innkeepers:	Joyce & Patrick Kennard
	Resident Owners
Open:	All Year
Facilities:	6 Bedrooms
	4 Private Baths, 1 Shared
Breakfast:	Gourmet
Rates:	$75 - $100 For 2 Guests
Payment:	MC,Visa,Check

Magnolia House, restored in 1991, was designed and built in 1923 for the Stein family. Edward Stein was the architect, head of the household and designer of the Gillespie County Courthouse. He selected each piece of lumber personally for the home, making it one of the most carefully constructed houses in this historic area.

Each of the six guest rooms in Magnolia House is uniquely decorated with antique furnishings. The Magnolia Suite features a Queen size bed and large comfortable living area with gas log fireplace and oak floor, has a private bath/shower and its own separate entrance. The Bluebonnet Suite has a living room, wood-burning fireplace, complete kitchen, mahogany King size bed, private bath with antique footed tub and a private entrance. The American Beauty Room offers a King size bed, antique dressing table, and private bath. The Peach Blossom Room has a Queen size bed, antique dressing table, stenciled ceiling trim and private bath. The Lili Marleen Room is a grand room on the main level with beautiful long-leaf yellow pine floor, King size bed, triple dresser with double mirror.

Each morning guests convene in the dining room to enjoy a full Southern breakfast prepared from scratch. Thoughtful amenities such as fresh flowers, home-brewed coffee, complimentary wine in the evenings, and monogrammed terrycloth robes make this bed and breakfast a luxurious retreat.

Smoking is limited to outside the house. Pets are not allowed. Check with hosts regarding children. Reservations are required. Ask about discounts.

Directions: From Main Street, go 7 blocks North on Llano Street (Hwy 16N), turn Left on Hackberry to house.

Member: PAII, Historical Assoc. of Texas

MITCHELL'S GUEST HOUSE

Ranch Rd 1376 At #1888
Fredericksburg 78624
Reservations: 210 997 5521/210 997 2759

Innkeepers:	Jym & Jan Mitchell
	Resident Owners
Open:	All Year
Facilities:	2 Bedrooms, All Private Baths
Breakfast:	Continental
Rates:	$59 - $79 For 2 Guests
Payment:	Check

In the heart of the Hill Country, Mitchell's Guest House, located two miles South of Luckenbach at the intersection of Ranch Roads 1376 and 1888, is just twelve minutes from downtown Fredericksburg. Guests can sit on the back porch and watch the wildlife and enjoy the wonderful view.

There are two separate apartments at this bed and breakfast. The downstairs apartment has an antique parlor, a full-sized, modern kitchen, a bathroom with a large tub and shower, two Queen size beds and lots of closet space. The upstairs apartment has two full size beds, a large walk-in closet, a bathroom with a shower and an efficiency kitchen.

A Continental breakfast will include pastries and breads from one of Fredericksburg's authentic German bakeries and homemade jams /jellies.

Reservations are necessary. Smoking is allowed outside only. Children are accommodated easily, but there are no provisions for pets.

Just ask Hosts Jym and Jan Mitchell for directions or recommendations on local fare and entertainment available. They will be happy to help make your stay more enjoyable.

Enjoy a quiet country atmosphere while staying at Mitchell's Guest House. Guests might even want to visit Luckenbach (population 25) which was settled in 1850 by German pioneers. This tiny hamlet was bought in the 1970's by the late Hondo Crouch, pixieish Hill Country humorist, writer and authentic Texas character. Sunday afternoon visitors to this tiny town are often treated to "happenings" when fiddlers, strummers and Banjo pickers form impromptu groups.

KEEPSAKE KOTTAGE

112 N. Acorn
Fredericksburg 78624
Reservations: 210 997 0205

Innkeeper:	Carolyn Moore, Resident Owner
Open:	All Year
Facilities:	1 Bedroom, 1 Bath Cottage
Breakfast:	Continental
Rates:	$85 For 2 Guests
Payment:	Check

LOST CREEK BED & BREAKFAST

Highway 16, 5 Mi. South Of Main St
Fredericksburg 78624
Reservations: 210 997 0774

Innkeepers:	Ernie & Billie Vieluf, Resident Owners
Open:	All Year
Facilities:	2 Bedrooms, 1 Shared Bath
Breakfast:	Continental Plus
Rates:	$106 - $111 For 2 Guests
Payment:	MC,Visa,Check

MAIN STREET BED & BREAKFAST

337 E. Main
Fredericksburg 78624
Reservations: 210 997 0153/800 666 5548

Innkeepers:	Bill, Sharon & Jennifer Grona Resident Owners
Open:	All Year
Facilities:	4 Suites With Private Baths
Breakfast:	Continental Plus
Rates:	$85 - $99 For 2 Guests
Payment:	All Major,Check

OLD RANCH HOMEPLACE

HC 61, Box 114
Fredericksburg 78624
Reservations: 210 997 5476

Innkeeper:	Carolyn Ellebracht, Resident Owner
Open:	Seasonal - April to December
Facilities:	2 Bedrooms, 1 Shared Bath
Breakfast:	Full
Rates:	$55 - $100 For 2 Guests
Payment:	Check

RESSMANN-WAGEN HAUS COMPLEX

104 E. Schubert
Fredericksburg 78624
Reservations: 210 685 3163/210 991 5612

Innkeepers:	Bill & HelenTeague, Resident Owners
Open:	All Year
Facilities:	4 Bedrooms, All Pvt Baths Plus 1Bed-1bath Cottage
Breakfast:	OYO
Rates:	$77 - $95 For 2 Guests
Payment:	MC,Visa,Disc,Check

ROCKY TOP BED & BREAKFAST

Highway 965, 8 Mi. North Of Main St
Fredericksburg 78624
Reservations: 210 997 8145

Innkeeper:	Susan Creenwelge, Resident Owner
Open:	All Year
Facilities:	4 Bedrooms, 1 Pvt Bath, 2 Shared-
Breakfast:	OYO
Rates:	$60 - $70 For 2 Guests
Payment:	Check

SUNNYSIDE PROPERTIES B&B

714 W. Creekside
Fredericksburg 78624
Reservations: 210 997 3049

Innkeepers:	John & Pat Hoggard, Owners
Open:	All Year
Facilities:	Varied - See Next Page
Breakfast:	Continental
Rates:	$70 - $85 For 2 Guests
Payment:	MC,Visa,Disc,Check

Sunnyside Properties offers you a choice of seven different accommodations:

Almost Heaven - 412 West Austin
A two bedroom, one bath house. Continental breakfast included. $85 double occupancy.

Longhorn Corral - 207 South Bowie
A three bedroom, one bath home. Continental breakfast included. $85 double occupancy.

Sleepy Hollow - 714 West Creek
A one bedroom, one bath house. Continental breakfast included. $70 double occupancy.

Sunnyside Cottage - 114 North Crockett
A two bedroom, one bath home. Continental breakfast included. $70 double occupancy.

Sunnyside Haus - 412 West Austin
A two bedroom, one bath home. Continental breakfast included. $85 double occupancy.

Sunnyside Manor - 211 North Crockett
A two bedroom, one bath home. Continental breakfast included. $80 double occupancy.

Western Star - 207 South Bowie
A three bedroom, one bath home. Continental breakfast included. $85 double occupancy.

Smoking is not allowed in these facilities. No children or pets. Reservations are required. Golf facility nearby.

Directions: All properties close to downtown Fredericksburg

Member: Historic Hotel Association of Texas

RUSTIC LOFT BED & BREAKFAST

414 E. Main
Fredericksburg 78624
Reservations: 210 997 6219

Innkeepers:	Rodney & Sharon Smajstrla
	Resident Owners
Open:	All Year
Facilities:	1 Bedroom With Bath
Breakfast:	OYO
Rates:	$75 For 2 Guests
Payment:	MC,Visa,Check

SCHMIDT BARN BED & BREAKFAST

1.5 Mi West Of Town
Fredericksburg 78624
Reservations: 210 997 5612

Innkeepers:	Charles & Loreta Schmidt
	Resident Owners
Open:	All Year
Facilities:	1 Bedroom - 1 Bath Guest House
Breakfast:	Full
Rates:	$77 For 2 Guests
Payment:	MC,Visa,Disc,Check

SETTLERS CROSSING
HISTORIC GUEST HOUSES

Settler Crossing Rd
Fredericksburg 78624
Reservations: 210 997 5612/210 997 2722

Innkeepers:	David & Judy Bland, Resident Owners
Open:	All Year
Facilities:	Four 1 Bedrrom, 1 Bath Houses
Breakfast:	Continental Plus
Rates:	$79 - $110 For 2 Guests
Payment:	All Major,Check

TEXAS STAR BED & BREAKFAST

290 West & Royal Oaks Dr West
Fredericksburg 75023
Reservations: 210 997 5612

Innkeeper:	Mrs. C. W. Rogers
Open:	All Year
Facilities:	1 Bedroom With Bath
Breakfast:	Continental Plus
Rates:	$72 For 2 Guests
Payment:	MC,Visa,Disc,Check

THE BACK FORTY OF FREDERICKSBURG

1311 Bob Moritz Dr
Fredericksburg 78624
Reservations: 210 997 6373

Innkeeper:	Pat Collins, Resident Owner
Open:	All Year
Facilities:	2 Bedrooms, All Private Baths
Breakfast:	Continental Plus
Rates:	$100 For 2 Guests
Payment:	Check

THE COTTAGE

415 B Plum
Fredericksburg 78624
Reservations: 512 552 2800/210 997 6906

Innkeeper:	Diane Weeks, Resident Owner
Open:	All Year
Facilities:	1 Bedroom, 1 Bath Cottage
Breakfast:	OYO
Rates:	$70 For 2 Guests
Payment:	Check

TEXAS TWO-STEP BED & BREAKFAST

509 N. Cherry
Fredericksburg 78624
Reservations: 210 997 2407/210 997 5612

Innkeeper: Anne Weigers, Resident Owner
Open: All Year
Facilities: 1 Bedroom With Bath
Breakfast: Gourmet
Rates: $125 For 2 Guests
Payment: All Major,Check

If romance and luxury are what you're looking for then Texas Two-Step is the place for you. Located only three blocks from Main Street, but outside the city limits, it features a charming Sunday House in a country setting.

Antiques, wonderful art, an open fireplace, TV and game table (with games galore) welcome you into the living room.

An 1853 Mallsod bed which has been in your hostess' family since that time, is the highlight of the gigantic bedroom. Beyond is a huge bath with a tub-for-two and a shower-for-two. Overhead is a skylight for moon and star-gazing from your bubble bath.

A full (and romantic! . . . How about heart-shaped waffles) breakfast is delivered to your charming kitchen/dining area the night before so that you can enjoy the feast at your leisure when the spirit moves you.

Complimentary wine is provided to guests celebrating anniversaries, birthdays or on their honeymoon.

This guesthouse accommodates two non-smoking adults. Pets are not allowed. Reservations are required.

Directions: Three blocks north of Main Street

THE HERB HAUS BED & BREAKFAST
402 Whitney Street
Fredericksburg 78624
Reservations: 210 997 8615/800 259 Herb

Innkeepers:	Bill & Silvia Varney, Resident Owners
Open:	All Year
Facilities:	2 Bedroom - 1 Bath Guest House
Breakfast:	Continental Plus
Rates:	$95 For 2 Guests
Payment:	All Major,Check

THE SPRING LOG HAUS
R. Road 2721
Fredericksburg 78624
Reservations: 210 997 5671

Innkeepers:	Guenther & LaVerne Ottmers Owner/Manager
Open:	Seasonal - January to October
Facilities:	2 Bedroom, 1 Pvt Bath, 1 Shared
Breakfast:	OYO
Rates:	$95 For 2 Guests
Payment:	MC,Visa,Amex,Check

THE VERRANDA
301 E. Centre St.
Fredericksburg 78624
Reservations: 210 997 8948

Innkeepers:	Rodney & Sue Seay, Resident Owners
Open:	All Year
Facilities:	4 Room Suite, 1 Pvt Bath, 1 Shared
Breakfast:	Full
Rates:	$75 - $95 For 2 Guests
Payment:	Check

VOGEL SUNDAY HOUSE

418 W. Austin
Fredericksburg 78624
Reservations: 210 997 5612/997 7135

Innkeepers:	King & Marilynne Ransom
	Resident Owners
Open:	All Year
Facilities:	1 Bedroom, 1 Bath Suite
Breakfast:	Gourmet
Rates:	$67 For 2 Guests
Payment:	MC,Visa,Disc,Check

WATKINS HILL GUEST HOUSE

608 E. Creek
Fredericksburg 78624
Reservations: 210 997 6739

Innkeeper:	Edgar Watkins, Resident Owner
Open:	All Year
Facilities:	3 Bedrooms, All Private Baths
Breakfast:	Gourmet
Rates:	$100 - $140 For 2 Guests
Payment:	MC,Visa,Check

WOLF CREEK BARN

16 Mi. South Of Town On Highway 16
Fredericksburg 78624
Reservations: 210 997 5612

Innkeeper:	E. King, Owner
Open:	All Year
Facilities:	1 Bedroom, 1 Bath
Breakfast:	OYO
Rates:	$98 For 2 Guests
Payment:	MC,Visa,Disc,Check

Freeport

ANCHOR BED & BREAKFAST

342 Anchor Drive
Freeport 77541
Reservations: 409 239 3543

Innkeepers:	Elliott & Kathy Loy
	Resident Owners
Open:	All Year
Facilities:	2 Bedrooms, 1 Bath
	Plus Dorm Room
Breakfast:	Continental OYO
Rates:	$45 - $65 For 2 Guests
Payment:	All Major

A newly constructed bed and breakfast in the Treasure Island Subdivision at San Luis Pass, Anchor Bed & Breakfast hosts, Elliott and Kathy Loy, say "our guests are like personal friends and we take real good care to make their stay with us an enjoyable one, something to tell their friends about".

This waterfront bed and breakfast features prime fishing from a private pier on Cold Pass and private boat docking with deep channel access.

There are two beautiful suites with a common bath and a dorm room which accommodates four guests. Fresh flowers are always in the guests rooms.

Continental Plus breakfast is offered to guests whether they are early or late risers. Lunch and dinner from the grill are available at an extra charge.

Amenities include indoor sauna bathing overlooking the water. Enjoy an afternoon in the local area boasting beautiful clean beaches, superb seafood and steak restaurants, and live entertainment night life.

Children must be twelve years old, and small pets are accepted. Provisions for the handicapped. Reservations are required.

Senior citizen rates and off season rates are available as well as special discounts for groups, business travelers and multiple night stays

Directions: Take 288 South from Houston to Freeport - Confirmed reservations will receive additional directions.

Member: Texas Hotel & Motel Assn, Chamber of Commerce

BANKER'S INN BED & BREAKFAST

224 West Park Avenue
Freeport 77541
Reservations: 409 233 4932

Innkeeper:	Bob Bass, Resident Owner
Open:	All Year
Facilities:	3 Bedrooms, 2 Shared Baths
Breakfast:	Full
Rates:	$75 - $95 For 2 Guests
Payment:	Check

 # Friendswood

BROWN HOUSE

312 South Friendswood Dr
Friendswood 77546
Reservations: 713 482 2802/800 959 2802

Innkeeper:	Sky Lyn Williams, Resident Owner
Open:	All Year
Facilities:	7 Bedrooms, 5 Pvt Baths, 1 Shared
Breakfast:	Gourmet
Rates:	$65 - $120 For 2 Guests
Payment:	MC,Visa,Check

 **Fulton**

THE RODMAKER'S HOUSE

5030 N. Highway 35
Fulton 78358
Reservations: 512 790 8145

Innkeepers:	Dennis & Patsy Freeman
	Resident Owners
Open:	All Year
Facilities:	3 Bedrooms, All Private Baths
Breakfast:	Full
Rates:	$72.80 For 2 Guests
Payment:	MC,Visa,Check

 **Galveston**

CAROUSEL INN BED & BREAKFAST

712 10th Street
Galveston 77550
Reservations: 409 762 2166

Innkeepers:	Jim & Kathy Hughes, Resident Owners
Open:	All Year
Facilities:	4 Bedrooms, All Private Baths
Breakfast:	Continental Plus
Rates:	$85 - $110 For 2 Guests
Payment:	MC,Visa,Amex,Check

COPPERSMITH INN

1914 Avenue M
Galveston 77550
Reservations: 409 763 7004/713 965 7273

Innkeeper:	Lisa Hering, Resident Owner
Open:	All Year
Facilities:	5 Bedrooms, 2 Pvt Baths, 3 Shared
Breakfast:	Full On Weekends
Rates:	$85 - $135 For 2 Guests
Payment:	All Major,Check

HAZLEWOOD HOUSE BED & BREAKFAST

1127 Church Street
Galveston 77553
Reservations: 409 762 1668

Innkeepers:	Pat Hazlewood, Resident Owner
Open:	All Year
Facilities:	3 Bedrooms, All Private Baths
Breakfast:	Continental Plus
Rates:	$55 - $150 For 2 Guests
Payment:	Check

INN ON THE STRAND

2021 Strand
Galveston 77550
Reservations: 409 762 4444

Innkeepers:	Don & Carol Craig, Managers
Open:	All Year
Facilities:	6 Bedrooms With Private Baths
Breakfast:	Full
Rates:	$115 - $150 For 2 Guests
Payment:	MC,Visa,Amex

MICHAEL'S BED AND BREAKFAST
1715 35th Street
Galveston 77550
Reservations: 800 776 8302

Innkeeper:	Mikey Isbell, Resident Owner
Open:	All Year
Facilities:	4 Bedrooms, 1 Shared Bath
Breakfast:	Gourmet
Rates:	$85 For 2 Guests
Payment:	MC,Visa,Check

THE GILDED THISTLE BED & BREAKFAST
1805 Broadway
Galveston 77550
Reservations: 409 763 0194/800 654 9380

Innkeepers:	Helen & Pat Henemann
	Resident Owners
Open:	All Year
Facilities:	3 Bedrooms, 1 Pvt Bath, 1 Shared
Breakfast:	Full
Rates:	$145 - $165 For 2 Guests
Payment:	MC,Visa,Disc,Check

THE QUEEN ANNE BED & BREAKFAST
1915 Sealy
Galveston 77550
Reservations: 409 763 7088/800 472 0930

Innkeepers:	John McWilliams & Earl French
	Resident Owners
Open:	All Year
Facilities:	5 Bedrooms, 2 Shared Baths
Breakfast:	Full
Rates:	$85 - $125 For 2 Guests
Payment:	MC,Visa,Amex,Check

MADAME DYER'S BED & BREAKFAST

1720 Postoffice Street
Galveston 77550
Reservations: 409 765 5692

Innkeepers:	Linda & Larry Bonnin
	Resident Owners
Open:	All Year
Facilities:	3 Bedrooms, All Private Baths
Breakfast:	Full
Rates:	$85 - $125 for 2 Guests
Payment:	MC,Visa,Check

Madame Dyer's Bed and Breakfast is conveniently located within walking distance of the Stand Historic District and the East End Historical home district, which is one of the most beautiful and best preserved area of Victorian homes in the country. Built in 1889, this two story home with wrap around porches is a classic example of Victorian architecture adapted to suit Galveston's climate.

All rooms offer bathrobes, ceiling fans, bicycles, access to porches, wooden floors with area rugs and lace curtains. On the second floor, there are three bedrooms to accommodate guests: Ashten's Room is furnished with a Queen size bed of carved oak along with other antique pieces and accents to make a truly elegant room. Blake's Room, furnished in English antiques with a full size bed set in a bay window and a delicately crocheted bedspread includes a private bath with a deep claw footed tub. Corbin's Room features twin poster beds complimented by a tiled fireplace with an oak mantel. Antique dolls, whimsical old hats and floral swags adorn this delightful room.

Guests will find fresh ground brewed coffee located on an antique buffet upstairs for the early riser. A full breakfast is served in the formal dining room where the fragrance of steaming coffee, breakfast breads, cereals, fruit and juice whet the appetite for the homemade "specialty of the day". Afternoon tea, snacks and beverages are provided.

No pets or small children are allowed; however, teenagers are welcome. Smoking is not permitted indoors although ashtrays are provided on the porches. Reservations are suggested. Inquire about senior citizen rates and extended stays.

Member: Professional Assn of Innkeepers Int'l, Texas Hotel/Motel Assoc.

THE VICTORIAN BED & BREAKFAST INN
511 17th Street
Galveston 77550
Reservations: 409 762 3235

Innkeeper:	Marcy Hanson, Resident Manager
Open:	All Year
Facilities:	2 Bedroom Suites With Pvt Bath
	3 Bedrooms With 1.5 Shared Baths
Breakfast:	Continental Plus
Rates:	$85 - $200 For 2 Guests
Payment:	MC,Visa,Amex,Check

TRUBE CASTLE INN
1627 Sealy Ave
Galveston 77550
Reservations: 409 765 4396/800 662 9647

Innkeeper:	Nonette O'Donnel, Resident Owner
Open:	All Year Except Christmas
Facilities:	2 Suites With Private Baths
Breakfast:	Full
Rates:	$125 - $195 For 2 Guests
Payment:	All Major,Check

 **Garland**

CATNAP CREEK BED & BREAKFAST
417 Glen Canyon Dr
Garland 75040
Reservations: 214 298 8586

Innkeepers:	Gene & Nancy Cushion,Owners
Open:	All Year
Facilities:	1 Bedroom With Bath
Breakfast:	Full
Rates:	$38 For 2 Guests
Payment:	MC,Visa,Check

 **Georgetown**

HISTORIC PAGE HOUSE

1000 Leander Road
Georgetown 78628
Reservations: 512 863 8979

Innkeeper:	Paula Arand, Resident Owner
Open:	All Year
Facilities:	6 Bedrooms, All Private Baths
Breakfast:	Full
Rates:	$75 - $85 For 2 Guests
Payment:	MC,Visa,Check

MORSE'S COUNTRY COTTAGE

40001 Heritage Hollow
Georgetown 78626
Reservations: 512 863 3117

Innkeepers:	Robert & Joanne Morse, Owners
Open:	All Year
Facilities:	1 Bedroom - 1 Bath Cottage
Breakfast:	Tailored To Guest
Rates:	$65 For 2 Guests
Payment:	Cash Only

HARPER-CHESSHER HISTORIC INN

1309 College Street
Georgetown 78626
Reservations: 512 863 4057

Innkeepers:	Jan Dobrozyski & Chris Golding Resident Managers
Open:	All Year
Facilities:	5 Bedrooms, All Private Baths
Breakfast:	Continental Plus
Rates:	$70 - $95 For 2 Guests
Payment:	MC,Visa,Amex,Check

CLAIBOURNE HOUSE

912 Forest
Georgetown 78626
Reservations: 512 930 3934

Innkeeper:	Clare Easley, Resident Owner
Open:	All Year
Facilities:	4 Bedrooms, All Private Baths
Breakfast:	Continental Plus
Rates:	$85 - $95 For 2 Guests
Payment:	MC,Visa,Check

Located three blocks West of Historic Square which is cited on the National Register of Historic Places, Claibourne House is in the heart of "old Georgetown". Built in 1896, this spacious Victorian was restored in 1987 and adapted for use as a bed and breakfast.

Owner and hostess Clare Easley, a native of the area, is pleased to offer day tour suggestions and give guests the names of a few good restaurants. Of interest certainly is Texas' newest and most accessible subterranean cavern on I-35 just South of town where the temperature is a constant 72 degrees year round.

Guests are accommodated in four bedrooms, each with a private bath. An intimate upstairs sitting room and downstairs grand hall, parlor and wrap-around porch are available to guests. The guest rooms are handsomely furnished with treasured family furniture, antiques and fine art.

Continental Plus breakfast fare is offered to guests as well as a welcoming glass of wine.

Smoking is permitted on porches. The bed and breakfast can accommodate children over twelve years of age. Inquire about bringing pets. Reservations are required. Extended stay discounts are offered.

Directions: I-35 to Hwy 29 exit. East to second red light and turn Left two blocks to 10th Street. Left two more blocks to 10th and Forest and you're there!

Member: Professional Assn of Innkeepers International.

Geroge West

COUNTRY ESTATES BED & BREAKFAST
Highway 59, 9 Mi. W. Of Georgetown
Geroge West 78022
Reservations: 512 566 2335

Innkeepers:	Fred & Evelyn Johnson
	Resident Owners
Open:	All Year
Facilities:	3 Bedrooms, 1 Pvt Bath, 2 Shared
Breakfast:	Full
Rates:	$75 - $85 For 2 Guests
Payment:	Check

Gladewater

CAROUSEL HOUSE BED & BREAKFAST
301 W. Commerce
Gladewater 75647
Reservations: 903 845 6830

Innkeeper:	Annette Wilson, Resident Owner
Open:	All Year
Facilities:	10 Bedrooms, All Private Baths
Breakfast:	Full
Rates:	$45 - $55 For 2 Guests
Payment:	MC,Visa,Amex,Check

HONEYCOMB SUITES BED & BAKERY

111 North Main Street
Gladewater 75647
Reservations: 903 845 2448

Innkeepers:	Bill & Susan Morgan, Resident Owners
Open:	All Year
Facilities:	7 Bedrooms, All Private Baths
Breakfast:	Gourmet
Rates:	$75 - $130 For 2 Guests
Payment:	All Major,Check

ROSE COTTAGE BED AND BREAKFAST ON THE LAKE

1620 West Lake Drive
Gladewater 75647
Reservations: 903 758 2290

Innkeepers:	Dell & Ernie Bunata, Absent Hosts
Open:	All Year
Facilities:	2 Bedroom, 1 Bath Cottage
Breakfast:	OYO
Rates:	$100 For 2 Guests
Payment:	MC,Visa,Check

Glen Rose

HUMMINGBIRD LODGE

Rt. 1, Box 496A
Glen Rose 76043
Reservations: 817 897 2787

Innkeepers:	Richard & Sherry Fowlkes
	Resident Owners
Open:	All Year
Facilities:	6 Bedrooms
	5 Private Baths, 1 Shared
Breakfast:	Continental Plus
Rates:	$75 - $95 For 2 Guests
Payment:	MC,Visa,Check

Come find the trees and steams, the deer and the birds, the peace and quiet at Hummingbird Lodge, all 144 wooded acres of it, in the hills of Somervell Country, Texas, just 70 miles Southwest of the center of the Dallas/Fort worth Metropolitan Area. Native cedar brakes and spreading oak groves, flowing with crystal clear streams beckon you to kick back, relax and restore yourself.

Hide away in a comfortable guest room furnished with antiques and country furniture. Picnic in the woods. Retreat to the cozy library with a book, audio tape or video. Meet and visit with other guests in the living room, dining room or at the secluded hot tub. Enjoy birding in the woods and fields or by Frog Spring Pond, on this major flyway. Walk or jog on The Pasture Trail. Hike and explore on The Woods Trail. Meditate or just daydream by the pond or by the waterfall. Study the ever expanding collection of native plants and grasses. Star gaze in the clear country night sky. Play volleyball, horseshoes or badminton. Bring your bike and explore paved country roads. Fish in the stocked pond.

Six guest rooms with private baths (two rooms share a shower). Four rooms have a refrigerator. The living room can serve as a private meeting room for eighteen; the dining room handles twenty. Both rooms have wood burning fireplaces. An ample Continental Plus breakfast is served to all guests.

The Lodge is a smoking-free facility. Regretfully they cannot accommodate guests under the age of 18 and have no facilities for pets. Reservations are required. Check in time is 3 p.m. and check out is at 11a.m. Special rates for over 55 seniors, for weekdays and off season. Provisions have been made for the handicapped. Golf facilities are nearby.

Member: PAII, ABBA, THMA

INN ON THE RIVER

205 S. W. Barnard St
Glen Rose 76043
Reservations: 214 424 7119

Innkeeper:	Kathi Thompson, Manager
Open:	All Year
Facilities:	22 Bedrooms, All Private Baths
Breakfast:	Gourmet
Rates:	$115 - $165 For 2 Guests
Payment:	All Major,Check

Relax under 200 year old oak trees in adirondack chairs that line the river banks at the Inn on the River. Located just 80 miles Southwest of Dallas, the inn offers casual elegance, a peaceful environment and gourmet meals. Inn on the River is a Texas historical landmark and the largest inn in Texas.

There are 22 guest rooms, each with its own private bath. Individually decorated with antiques, featherbeds and down comforters, guests are made to feel pampered and special. A large swimming pool is on site for a "dip".

The Inn's conference center offers a lodge atmosphere with a stone fireplace inside and out, open to a porch that overlooks the river. On the opposite side of the room, French doors allow the sunshine and fresh air to enter the room. This is a perfect place for corporate meetings and executive retreats anytime of the year. A complete meeting package (CMP) is offered by the Inn, including single occupancy accommodations, three gourmet meals, refreshment breaks and conference for $175/person per day.

Guests breakfast include such delights as Raspberry Banana Muffins, Hickory Smoked Bacon, Homemade Belgian Waffles with Fresh Peaches and Cream, Baked Eggs Florentine and, of course, fresh fruit. Afternoon tea is also available, upon request. Snacks and beverages are provided and guests may bring their own wine for that special occasion.

The Inn cannot accommodate smoking, children or pets. Reservations are required.

Member: Professional Innkeepers, American Bed & Breakfast Association, Meeting Planners International

YE OLE MAPLE INN

1509 Van Zandt
Glen Rose 76043
Reservations: 817 897 3456

Innkeeper:	Roberta Maple, Resident Owner
Open:	All Year
Facilities:	2 Bedrooms, All Private Baths
Breakfast:	Full
Rates:	$65 - $75 For 2 Guests
Payment:	MC,Visa,Check

Overlooking the serene Paluxy River, Ye Ole Maple Inn, surrounded by a white picket fence and six large pecan trees (one rumored to be over 200 years old), exudes tranquillity. The original house on the site was replaced by this one in 1950, where guests can swing or rock on the front porch and let the world go by.

Antiques in the home include a grandfather clock from Germany, a collection of 20th Century salt cellars and Santa Clauses and a pre-Civil War brass clock. The bed and breakfast offers two bedrooms. One is done in a country decor of pink and gray with a white iron and brass Queen size bed. You can enjoy reading in the privacy of your room while sitting in the white wicker chairs. The adjoining bathroom boasts an old footed tub. The second bedroom is done in Victorian decor of forest green and white with a four poster Queen size bed. This room also has a private reading area and private bath.

Breakfast is served in the dining room between 8:30 and 9:00 a.m. and includes fresh fruit or fruit compote, orange juice and coffee or tea and an entree. Your hostess, Roberta Maple, has been known to serve such mouth-watering items as oatmeal pancakes with pecan sauce, maple baked eggs, and an egg/sausage/apple casserole. Desert is served to guests every evening, so get ready for such delights as chocolate decadent cake and peanut butter pie!!

The Inn cannot accommodate children under the age of 18, nor does it have facilities for pets. Smoking is allowed only on the porch. Reservations are required. Check in is after 3 p.m. and check out is at 11 a.m. Third night stay is half price. Provisions have been made for the handicapped. Your hostess presents a gift to birthday and anniversary guests.

Member: Texas Hotel/Motel Association

BUSSEY'S SOMETHING SPECIAL BED AND BREAKFAST

202 Hereford Street
Glen Rose 76043
Reservations: 817 897 4843

Innkeepers:	Susan & Morris Bussey, Owners
Open:	All Year
Facilities:	1 Bedroom Cottage With Bath
Breakfast:	OYO
Rates:	$70 - $80 For 2 Guests
Payment:	Check

INDIAN MOUNTAIN RANCH

18 Mi. South Of Town
Glen Rose 76043
Reservations: 817 796 4060

Innkeeper:	Vallie Taylor, Resident Owner
Open:	All Year
Facilities:	3 Bedrooms, 2 Pvt Baths
Breakfast:	Full
Rates:	$75 - $110 For 2 Guests
Payment:	Check

POPEJOY HAUS BED & BREAKFAST

County Rd #321
Glen Rose 77043
Reservations: 817 897 3521

Innkeeper:	Klare Popejoy, Resident Owner
Open:	All Year
Facilities:	1 Bedroom With Private Bath
Breakfast:	Full
Rates:	$75 - $80 For 2 Guests
Payment:	MC,Visa,Check

THE LODGE AT FOSSIL RIM

6 Mi. North Of Town
Glen Rose 76043
Reservations: 817 897 7452

Innkeepers:	Janet & Paul Charlton, Managers
Open:	All Year
Facilities:	5 Bedrooms, 3 Pvt Baths, 1 Shared
Breakfast:	Gourmet
Rates:	$125 - $225 For 2 Guests
Payment:	All Major,Check

 **Gonzales**

ST. JAMES INN

723 St. James Street
Gonzales 78629
Reservations: 210 672 7066

Innkeepers:	J.R. & Ann Covert, Resident Owners
Open:	All Year
Facilities:	5 Bedrooms, 4 Pvt Baths, 1 Shared
Breakfast:	Gourmet
Rates:	$55 - $95 For 2 Guests
Payment:	MC, Amex,Check

THE HOUSTON HOUSE

621 E. St. George St
Gonzales 78629
Reservations: 210 672 6940/875 5643

Innkeepers:	Eugene & Diana Smith
	Resident Owners
Open:	All Year
Facilities:	3 Bedrooms, 2 Pvt Baths, 1 Shared
Breakfast:	Full
Rates:	$75 - $100 For 2 Guests
Payment:	MC,Visa,Amex,Check

 **Granbury**

DABNEY HOUSE BED & BREAKFAST
106 South Jones
Granbury 76048
Reservations: 817 579 1260

Innkeepers:	John & Gwenn Hurley, Owners
Open:	All Year
Facilities:	1 Suite & 3 BR, All Private Baths
Breakfast:	Full
Rates:	$50 - $105 For 2 Guests
Payment:	MC,Visa,Amex,Check

IRON HORSE INN BED & BREAKFAST
616 N. Thorp Springs Rd
Granbury 76048
Reservations: 817 579 5535

Innkeepers:	John & Pam Ragland, Resident Owners
Open:	All Year
Facilities:	5 Bedrooms, All Private Baths
Breakfast:	Full
Rates:	$75 - $130 For 2 Guests
Payment:	MC,Visa,Check

PEARL STREET INN BED & BREAKFAST
319 West Pearl St
Granbury 76048
Reservations: 817 279-Pink

Innkeeper:	Danette Hebda, Resident Owner
Open:	All Year
Facilities:	5 Bedrooms, All Private Baths
Breakfast:	Gourmet
Rates:	$59 - $98 For 2 Guests
Payment:	Check

THE CAPTAIN'S HOUSE BED & BREAKFAST

123 W. Doyle Street
Granbury 76048
Reservations: 817 579-Lake/817 579 6664

Innkeepers:	Bob & Julia Pannell, Resident Owners
Open:	All Year
Facilities:	2 Bedrooms, All Private Baths
Breakfast:	Full
Rates:	$78 - $88 For 2 Guests
Payment:	Check

THE DOYLE HOUSE BED & BREAKFAST ON THE LAKE

205 W. Doyle
Granbury 76048
Reservations: 817 573 6492

Innkeepers:	Patrick & Linda Stoll, Resident Owners
Open:	All Year
Facilities:	3 Bedrooms, All Private Baths
Breakfast:	Gourmet
Rates:	$80 - $115 For 2 Guests
Payment:	All Major, Check

THE VICTORIAN ROSE BED & BREAKFAST

216 West Pearl
Granbury 76048
Reservations: 817 579 9673/800 430 7673

Innkeeper:	Joyce Paige, Resident Owner
Open:	All Year
Facilities:	3 Bedrooms, All Private Baths
Breakfast:	Full
Rates:	$50 - $90 For 2 Guests
Payment:	MC,Visa,Check

 # Granite Shoals

LA CASITA BED & BREAKFAST
1908 Redwood Dr
Granite Shoals 78654
Reservations: 512 598 6443/512 598 6448

Innkeepers:	Joanne & Roger Scarborough
	Resident Owners
Open:	All Year
Facilities:	1 Bedroom Cottage With Bath
Breakfast:	Full
Rates:	$65 For 2 Guests
Payment:	Check

 # Harlingen

THE ROSS HAUS
Near Center Of Town
Harlingen 78550
Reservations: 210 425 1717

Innkeepers:	Darrel & Grace Johnson
	Owner/Managers
Open:	All Year
Facilities:	Four 1 Bedroom, 1 Bath Apts
Breakfast:	Continental Plus
Rates:	$81.50 For 2 Guests
Payment:	Check

RIO GRANDE VALLEY

Not really a valley but a alluvial plain that stretches along the Rio Grande at the state's Southern tip, this section of Texas is a popular recreation area. Mexico is just a bridge away and visitors like the bicultural influences of the area - the spicy bite of Mexican cuisine, the beat of Spanish guitars and the sound of the Spanish language mixed with everyday English.

Travelers love the quick trip to a foreign country where prized souvenirs might include hand-blown glass, wrought iron, embroidered Mexican shirts and dresses, ceramics, and unusual jewelry.

The valley is a popular place for Winter Texans during the winter months because of its mild climate and abundance of "things to do". Visitors love the Sabal Palm Grove Wildlife Sanctuary, one of the best preserved Sabal Palm forests in the U.S., where the National Audubon Society has self-guided tours. Birding is at its best due to the many species of birds whom make this area their wintering grounds.

In Pharr visitors can view 2,000 antique clocks dating back to 1690 including many unusual and beautiful specimens at the Old Clock Museum. Of course you will want to spend some time on South Padre Island where parasailing, windsurfing, fishing, surfing and other water sports are available. Rodeo fans don't want to miss the Sheriff's Posse Rodeo every Saturday evening at rodeo arena two miles south of Edinburg.

Like cactus? View five acres of exotic and native cacti and succulents at the Sunderland Cactus Garden just North of Alamo.

Haskell

THE BEVERS HOUSE
ON BRICK STREET

311 North Avenue F
Haskell 79521
Reservations: 817 864 3284/800 580 3284

Innkeepers:	Abe & Ruby Turner
	Resident Owners
Open:	All Year
Facilities:	4 Bedrooms
	1 Pvt Bath, 2 Shared
Breakfast:	Full
Rates:	$50 For 2 Guests
Payment:	MC, Visa, Check

The Historical Bevers House on Brick Street was built in 1904 by Spence Bevers, an early contractor who built the home for his family with loving care and a quality seldom found in present times. To quote a friend who helped him build the house, "if he saw one board with a knot in it, he would throw it out."

Several families have owned this property over the year until Abe and Ruby Turner acquired the house in 1964 from Dr. R. A. Middleton, a local physician. The home was then extensively remodeled with an eye to retaining the essence of yesteryear. Guests enter a home filled with Colonial American antiques that have been collected over the years. The backyard features a swimming pool and a hot tub complemented by outdoor antique memorabilia.

The home offers three bedrooms choices. The Paul Revere (double bed), the Benjamin Franklin (Queen bed) and the Benedict Arnold (Queen bed/trundle bed) upstairs and the Betsy Ross (Queen bed, fireplace and connection bath) downstairs.

A full country breakfast is served. Evening meals are available if requested at the time the reservation is made. Dinner includes mesquite cooked steak with all the trimmings!! The house is also available for teas, receptions and social functions. Complimentary snacks and beverages are provided to guests.

Reservations are not required. Areas for smoking are available.

Directions: Three blocks North of Courthouse Square, Hwy 277, one block West First Baptist Church.

Hemphill

SUNSET - SUNRISE BED & BREAKFAST

HC 52, Box 331
Hemphill 75948
Reservations: 409 579 3265

Innkeeper:	Genie Sloan, Resident Owner
Open:	All Year
Facilities:	3 Bedrooms
	1 Pvt Bath, 1 Shared
Breakfast:	Continental Plus
Rates:	$65 - $70 For 2 Guests
Payment:	Check

Sunset-Sunrise Bed and Breakfast, sitting on a peninsula with Lake Toledo Bend as its backyard, is a two story brick and cedar home built circa 1970. The home is a mixture of country and contemporary design with antique and eclectic furnishings. Ask your hostess, Genie Sloan, to point out some of the paintings, sculpture pieces and furniture that she purchased in France.

Guests can hire an experienced guide to "take you where the fish bite" or if hunting is your sport, there are guides aplenty for hire. However, if you would rather watch animals than shoot them, you may be lucky enough to spot a fox or a bobcat or a deer and its fawn. But, if all you want to do is relax, then that's okay too, for Genie's home is a serene oasis where you can forget the world.

Double occupancy guest bedrooms all have a view of the lake with one room opening to a balcony that's perfect for sunbathing. There is also a large pier from which to fish, sun bathe or tie up your boat.

Breakfast on the lake is continental and includes cold cereals, muffins, fresh fruit, toast, juice and coffee/tea. The choice of the lighter morning meal in contrast to the heavier American one is probably because Genie is accustomed to life overseas, having lived and traveled extensively in Europe. There is probably a story behind the 10 foot "knight in shining armor" on the lawn, too!!

Smoking is permitted in the yard only. Children and pets are not allowed. Reservations are required.

Directions: 15 miles South of Hemphill, off Highway 87. Turn at S.F. 2028 to end of blacktop, proceed 2.5 miles to B&B.

Member: Houston Society of Bed & Breakfasts, Sabine County Chamber of Commerce

# Hillsboro

JONES HOUSE BED & BREAKFAST
301 E. Franklin
Hillsboro 76645
Reservations: 817 582 0211/800 Jones-40

Innkeepers:	Paul & Claudia Jones, Resident Owner
Open:	All Year
Facilities:	3 Bedrooms, 1 Pvt Bath, 1 Shared
Breakfast:	Gourmet
Rates:	$52 - $65 For 2 Guests
Payment:	Check

TARLTON HOUSE OF 1895
BED & BREAKFAST
211 N. Pleasant
Hillsboro 76645
Reservations: 817 582 7216/800 823 7216

Innkeepers:	Mary & Eugene Smith
	Resident Owners
Open:	All Year
Facilities:	8 Bedrooms, All Private Baths
Breakfast:	Full
Rates:	$68 - $116 For 2 Guests
Payment:	MC,Visa,Amex,Check

 **Houston**

DURHAM HOUSE BED & BREAKFAST INN
921 Heights Blvd.
Houston 77008
Reservations: 713 868 4654

Innkeeper:	Marguerite Swanson, Resident Owner
Open:	All Year
Facilities:	6 Bedrooms, 4 Pvt Baths, 1 Shared
Breakfast:	Full
Rates:	$55 - $95 For 2 Guests
Payment:	All Major, Check

PATRICIAN BED & BREAKFAST INN
1200 Southmore Avenue
Houston 77004
Reservations: 713 523 1114/800 553 5797

Innkeeper:	Pat Thomas, Resident Owner
Open:	All Year
Facilities:	4 Bedrooms, All Private Baths
Breakfast:	Full
Rates:	$75 - $95 For 2 Guests
Payment:	All Major, Check

ROBIN'S NEST BED & BREAKFAST
4104 Greeley
Houston 77006
Reservations: 713 528 5821/800 622 8343

Innkeeper:	Robin Smith, Resident Owner
Open:	All Year
Facilities:	4 Bedrooms, All Private Baths
Breakfast:	Full
Rates:	$75 - $95 For 2 Guests
Payment:	All Major,Check

SARA'S BED & BREAKFAST INN
941 Heights Blvd
Houston 77008
Reservations: 713 868 1130/800 593 1130

Innkeepers:	Donna & Tillman Arledge
	Resident Owners
Open:	All Year
Facilities:	12 Bedrooms, 10 Pvt Baths, 2 Shared
Breakfast:	Continental Plus
Rates:	$55 - $95 For 2 Guests
Payment:	All Major,Check

THE HIGHLANDER BED & BREAKFAST
607 Highland Avenue
Houston 77009
Reservations: 713 861 6110

Innkeepers:	Arlen & Georgie McIrvin
	Resident Owners
Open:	All Year
Facilities:	4 Bedrooms, 3 Shared Baths
Breakfast:	Full
Rates:	$65 - $75 For 2 Guests
Payment:	All Major, Check

THE LOVETT INN
501 Lovett Blvd
Houston 77006
Reservations: 713 522 5224/800 779 5224

Innkeeper:	Tom Fricke, Resident Owner
Open:	All Year
Facilities:	8 Bedrooms, All Private Baths
Breakfast:	Continental Plus
Rates:	$65 - $125 For 2 Guests
Payment:	MC,Visa,Amex

WEBBER HOUSE BED & BREAKFAST

1011 Heights Blvd.
Houston 77008
Reservations: 713 864 9472

Innkeeper:	Joann Jackson, Resident Owner
Open:	All Year
Facilities:	4 Bedrooms, All Priviate Baths
Breakfast:	Full
Rates:	$75 - $110 For 2 Guests
Payment:	All Major,Check

Hunt

JOY SPRING RANCH BED & BREAKFAST

Rt. 1, Box 174A
Hunt 78024
Reservations: 512 238 4531

Innkeepers:	June & Don Price, Resident Owners
Open:	All Year
Facilities:	2 Room Cabin, 1 Pvt Bath, 1 Shared
Breakfast:	Full
Rates:	$60 - $75 For 2 Guests
Payment:	Check

RIVER BEND BED & BREAKFAST

FM1340
Hunt 78024
Reservations: 210 238 4681/800 472 3933

Innkeepers:	Conrad & Terry Pyle, Owners
	Becky Key, Manager
Open:	All Year
Facilities:	15 Bedrooms, All Private Baths
Breakfast:	Gourmet
Rates:	$85 - $115 For 2 Guests
Payment:	All Major, Check

Located in the heart of the Texas Hill Country on the beautiful Guadalupe River, River Bend Bed & Breakfast is a delight to the senses. Exquisite view of the scenic surroundings can be seen from all rooms and suites. The buildings are made from natural limestone with rough-hewn cedar accents. This retreat offers guests canoeing, swimming, tubing, fishing, and 55 acres of hiking,

The hardwood floors and antique fixtures in the main lodge accent the turn-of-the-century decor. Wrought-iron beds, lace curtains and footed tubs are in most rooms. Guests have a large selection of accommodations: Main Lodge: Six rooms with one double bed in each, one room with two twins, one room with a Queen bed. Each room has a private bath. Main Lodge Suites: There are two suites upstairs. Each suite has a double bed in one room and a daybed/trundle in the sitting room, private bath. Ranch House: Adjacent to the main lodge, this single story rock building has 3 units, side by side. One unit has two twins, one unit has a double and two twins and one unit has a double with a single. Hill House: Constructed the same as the Ranch House, it has two large rooms. Both have one double and two twin beds and a private bath.

Each morning you will wake up to the smell of freshly brewed coffee and other delicious aromas from the gourmet breakfast buffet. The main dish varies daily, but you can count on homemade breads/muffins and an abundant fruit plate.

Children under twelve are welcome in the Ranch and Hill House, but rooms in the Main Lodge are reserved for adults. Neither smoking nor pets are allowed. Reservations are recommended. Check in between 2-9 p.m. and check out is at 11 a.m. Ask about discounts and special packages.

Directions: 2.8 miles West of Hunt on FM 1340

Huntsville

THE WHISTLER BED & BREAKFAST

906 Avenue M
Huntsville 77340
Reservations: 409 295 2834/800 308 4016

Innkeeper:	Mary T. Clegg, Resident Owner
Open:	All Year
Facilities:	5 Bedrooms
	3 Private Baths, 1 Shared
Breakfast:	Gourmet
Rates:	$95 - $120 For 2 Guests
Payment:	Check

174

It you are looking for genuine Victorian elegance in a bed and breakfast, then The Whistler, sitting on three wooded acres, is a perfect setting for you. The house has been in the Thomason-Eastham family for five generations. Your hostess, Mary Thomason Clegg (who can satisfy any history-buffs curiosity), says that her great-great-uncle owned the property, and is credited with building the initial structure about 1859. Mary named her home "The Whistler" after her grandfather known for his melodious whistle.

Polished hardwood floors downstairs and pine floors upstairs complement such family antique furnishings as the walnut secretary circa 1850, an eleven foot tall sideboard made by penitentiary inmates, a rosewood table that was once a piano, several old family quilts and, of course, the five fireplaces.

The beautifully renovated two story home has five bedrooms available for guests, four upstairs and one downstairs. All have antique double or twin beds and their own complete private bathrooms. Common rooms include the formal reception room, music room, old-fashioned parlor, dining room and a spacious kitchen-family room combination.

Breakfast of a gourmet quality is served in a formal setting with china, silver and crystal. . . although guests like to gather for coffee on the East Terrace.

The bed and breakfast cannot accommodate children, pets or smoking.

Directions: Exit 116 off I-45 and go East on 11th Street for 1.2 miles. Turn Left onto FM 247 (Avenue M) to just past 9th street on your Left.

Member: Texas Family Land Heritage Register, Historical Accommodations of Texas

BLUE BONNET BED & BREAKFAST

1215 Avenue G, #4
Huntsville 77340
Reservations: 409 295 2072

Innkeepers:	John & Bette Nelson, Resident Owners
Open:	All Year
Facilities:	4 Bedrooms, 2 Pvt Baths, 1 Shared
Breakfast:	Continental Plus
Rates:	$40 - $50 For 2 Guests
Payment:	Check

LONGHORN HOUSE BED & BREAKFAST

Rt 1, Box 681
Huntsville 77342
Reservations: 409 295 1774/409 295 1844

Innkeeper:	Claire Jordan, Resident Owner
Open:	All Year
Facilities:	3 Bedrooms, 1 Shared Bath
Breakfast:	Full
Rates:	$65 - $75 For 2 Guests
Payment:	Check

 Ingram

RIVER OAKS LODGE BED & BREAKFAST

HCR 78, Box 231A
Ingram 78025
Reservations: 210 367 4214/800 608 2596

Innkeepers:	Gilda & Byron Wilkinson Resident Owners
Open:	All Year
Facilities:	6 Bedrooms, All Private Baths
Breakfast:	Gourmet
Rates:	$85 - $125 For 2 Guests
Payment:	MC,Check

 **Iraan**

PARKER RANCH BED & BREAKFAST

2.5 Mi. North Of Hwy 190 & CR 310
Iraan 79744
Reservations: 915 639 2850

Innkeeper:	Dickie Dell Ferro, Resident Owner
Open:	All Year
Facilities:	4 Bedrooms, 2 Pvt Baths, 1 Shared
Breakfast:	Continental Plus
Rates:	$50 For 2 Guests
Payment:	Check

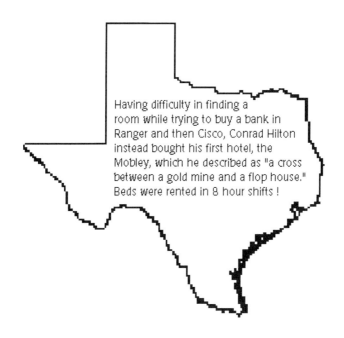

Having difficulty in finding a room while trying to buy a bank in Ranger and then Cisco, Conrad Hilton instead bought his first hotel, the Mobley, which he described as "a cross between a gold mine and a flop house." Beds were rented in 8 hour shifts !

Jacksboro

JACKSBORO COUNTRY INN
BED & BREAKFAST

112 West Belknap
Jacksboro 76458
Reservations: 817 567 3120/567 6600

Innkeepers:	John & Elaine Baen, Managers
Open:	All Year
Facilities:	12 Bedrooms
	1 Private Bath, 4 Shared
Breakfast:	Varies
Rates:	$65 For 2 Guests
Payment:	MC,Amex,Check

Jacksboro Country Inn Bed and Breakfast, built in 1921 and fully restored in 1994, is located in a town rich with Texas history. The two story structure is antique brick and features a collection of area game heads and fish from local ranches.

Among the many attractions is the restored Fort Richardson, abandoned in 1878, and now a historical site, or one can visit the Jack County Museum located in the oldest house in Jack County. The Jacksboro Country Inn hosts a big buck contest annually. Hunting and fishing trips can be arranged nearby, or bring your boat to use the two large new city lakes which have been fully stocked.

The Inn is furnished in "Old West Texas Cowboys and Indians", authentic antiques and collections of early Texas items. Custom cedar and four poster beds and other furniture crafted by Bill Bittle of Forestburg, Texas, add to the ambiance and comfort of guests.

This bed and breakfast has been featured in the Dallas Morning News, Texas Highways Magazine and many travel sections of various newspapers.

Guests have their choice of a Continental Plus, Full or OYO breakfast when making their reservations. Guests receive complimentary "all you can eat" Blue Bell Ice Cream at night before they tuck themselves into bed. (That would sweeten anyone's dreams!!)

Smoking is not permitted. Children are welcome but please leave pets at home. Handicapped facilities available. Reservations are recommended. Senior citizen rates are offered.

 Directions: Take 199 out of Ft. Worth to Jacksboro Courthouse. Go left ½ block on US 380 or take US 114 out of Dallas to Decatur. Go West on 114 - 380 to Jacksboro, left at Courthouse ½ block.

 # Jasper

THE BELL-JIM HOTEL
160 N. Austin
Jasper 75951
Reservations: 409 384 6923

Innkeepers:	Pat & David Stiles, Resident Owneres
Open:	All Year
Facilities:	8 Bedrooms, All Private Baths
Breakfast:	Full
Rates:	$50 For 2 Guests
Payment:	MC,Visa,Amex,Check

 # Jefferson

BLUEBONNET INN OF JEFFERSON
307 Soda Street
Jefferson 75657
Reservations: 903 665 8572

Innkeeper:	Sarah Williams, Resident Owner
Open:	All Year
Facilities:	2 Bedrooms, All Private Baths
Breakfast:	Full
Rates:	$85 For 2 Guests
Payment:	MC,Visa,Check

CAPTAIN'S CASTLE BED & BREAKFAST

403 East Walker
Jefferson 75657
Reservations: 903 665 2330

Innkeepers:	Barbara & Buck Hooker
	Resident Owners
Open:	All Year
Facilities:	7 Bedrooms, All Private Baths
Breakfast:	Full
Rates:	$85 - $100 For 2 Guests
Payment:	MC,Visa,Check

DIXON GUEST HOUSE

207 Dixon St
Jefferson 75657
Reservations: 903 665 8442

Innkeeper:	Joyce Jackson
Open:	All Year
Facilities:	3 Bedrooms, 1 Pvt Bath, 1 Shared
Breakfast:	Continental Plus
Rates:	$55 - $75 For 2 Guests
Payment:	Check

FALLING LEAVES INN

304 Jefferson St
Jefferson 75657
Reservations: 903 665 8803

Innkeepers:	Barbara & Joe Beu, Resident Owners
Open:	All Year
Facilities:	4 Bedrooms, All Private Baths
Breakfast:	Gourmet
Rates:	$75 - $100 For 2 Guests
Payment:	MC,Visa,Check

HALE HOUSE BED & BREAKFAST

702 S. Line St
Jefferson 75657
Reservations: 903 665 8877

Innkeeper:	Cherri Smith, Manager
Open:	All Year
Facilities:	7 Bedrooms, 3 Pvt Baths, 2 Shared
Breakfast:	Full
Rates:	$50 - $125 For 2 Guests
Payment:	MC,Visa,Check

HOLCOMB LODGE BED & BREAKFAST

Kim St. Lake O'the Pines
Jefferson 75657
Reservations: 903 665 3236

Innkeepers:	Glenda & Lex Holcomb, Managers
Open:	All Year
Facilities:	2 Bedrooms, 1 Bath
Breakfast:	OYO
Rates:	$50 - $115 For 2 Guests
Payment:	Check

HOME SWEET HOME LODGING

408 Soda St
Jefferson 75657
Reservations: 903 665 2493

Innkeepers:	Clarise & Ruben Penner Resident Owner
Open:	All Year
Facilities:	2 Bedrooms, All Private Baths
Breakfast:	Continental
Rates:	$50 - $75 For 2 Guests
Payment:	Check

MC KAY HOUSE BED & BREAKFAST INN

306 E. Delta St.
Jefferson 75657
Reservations: 903 665 7322/214 348 1922

Innkeepers:	Alma Anne & Joseph Parker, Managers
Open:	All Year
Facilities:	4 Bedrooms & 3 Suites, 7 Pvt Baths
Breakfast:	Gourmet
Rates:	$75 - $125 For 2 Guests
Payment:	MC,Visa,Check

PECAN PLACE BED & BREAKFAST

402 W. Lafayette
Jefferson 75657
Reservations: 903 665 8481

Innkeepers:	Cliff & Anna Bode, Owners
Open:	All Year
Facilities:	4 Suites, All Private Baths
Breakfast:	Continental Plus
Rates:	$55 - $85 For 2 Guests
Payment:	MC,Visa,Amex,Check

PRIDE HOUSE BED & BREAKFAST

409 Broadway
Jefferson 75657
Reservations: 903 665 2675

Innkeeper:	Ruthmary Jordan, Resident Owner
Open:	All Year
Facilities:	10 Bedrooms, All Private Baths
Breakfast:	Full
Rates:	$65 - $100 For 2 Guests
Payment:	MC,Visa,Check

MAISON BAYOU:
A CREOLE PLANTATION

300 Rue Bayou
Jefferson 75657
Reservations: 903 665 7600

Innkeepers:	Jan & Pete Hochendel
	Resident Owners
Open:	All Year
Facilities:	8 Bedrooms, All Private Baths
Breakfast:	Full
Rates:	$85 - $150 For 2 Guests
Payment:	MC, Visa, Check

Maison-Bayou: A Creole Plantation is located on the ancient riverbed of the Big Cypress in the midst of 55 wooded acres, yet is only a short walk or drive to the center of Historic Downtown Jefferson. The main house is an authentic reproduction of an 1850's Plantation Overseer's House which features Heart of Pine floors, pine walls and ceilings, natural gas burning lanterns in each room and period antiques and fabrics.

The Cabins are architecturally styled after authentic Slave Quarter Cabins where guests can relax with total privacy. Each cabin mixes primitive furnishings and modern conveniences to provide a perfect blend. All cabins have private baths, three feature a claw foot tub with brass hand-held shower. Another offers a large, handicapped accessible stand-up shower. The cabins are all located on the Cypress Beaver Pond with a full view.

One cabin even features a back deck, pier, dock and row boat for its guests exclusive use. Some cabins are built "Dog Trot" style, with two independent cabins, having a common roofline and sharing a full length front and back porch, but separated by a six foot breezeway which make them perfect for families yet private enough for couples.

Guests may enjoy fishing in either the Beaver Pond or along the 2000 foot of riverfront on Big Cypress Bayou. (No fishing license is required!!)

Smoking outside only. Boarding facilities for pets are available in town with advanced reservations. Children are welcome. Reservations are required Additional charges for extra guests in rooms. Two night minimum during festival and holiday dates.

Directions: Cross bridge from historic downtown Jefferson, then right on Bayou Street

Member: Texas Hotel/Motel Assn, Marion County Chamber & Jefferson Merchants Assn

ROSEVILLE MANOR
217 W. Lafayette
Jefferson 75657
Reservations: 903 665 2528

Innkeepers:	Harold & Charlotte Dial Simms
	Resident Owners
Open:	All Year
Facilities:	6 Bedrooms, All Private Baths
Breakfast:	Restaurant Voucher
Rates:	$60 - $95 For 2 Guests
Payment:	Check

SECRETS OF LAKE CLARBORN
BED & BREAKFAST
Hwy 59 North
Jefferson 75657
Reservations: 903 665 8518

Innkeeper:	Lois Smith, Resident Owner
Open:	All Year
Facilities:	2 Bedrooms, All Private Baths
Breakfast:	Full
Rates:	$75 For 2 Guests
Payment:	Check

THE FADED ROSE BED & BREAKFAST
1101 S. Line Street
Jefferson 75657
Reservations: 903 665 2716

Innkeeper:	Merlene Meek, Resident Owner
Open:	All Year
Facilities:	2 Bedrooms, All Private Baths
Breakfast:	Full
Rates:	$65 For 2 Guests
Payment:	Check

THE GINGERBREAD HOUSE/HONEY DO INN

601 E. Jefferson St
Jefferson 75657
Reservations: 903 665 8994

Innkeepers:	Norma & Douglas Horn
	Resident Owner
Open:	All Year
Facilities:	3 Suites With Private Baths
Breakfast:	Full
Rates:	$70 - $85 For 2 Guests
Payment:	MC,Visa,Check

THE PACE HOUSE BED & BREAKFAST

402 N. Polk St.
Jefferson 75657
Reservations: 903 665 1433/800 850 1433

Innkeeper:	Geraldine Pace Mason
	Resident Owner
Open:	All Year
Facilities:	2 Bedrooms, All Private Baths
Breakfast:	Gourmet
Rates:	$75 - $80 For 2 Guests
Payment:	MC,Visa,Disc,Check

THE SEASONS GUEST HOUSE
BED & BREAKFAST

409 South Alley
Jefferson 75657
Reservations: 903 665 1218

Innkeepers:	Kirby & Cindy Childress
	Resident Owners
Open:	All Year
Facilities:	3 Bedrooms, All Private Baths
Breakfast:	Gourmet
Rates:	$115 - $125 For 2 Guests
Payment:	MC,Visa,Check

TURNER HOUSE BED & BREAKFAST

210 E. Henderson
Jefferson 75657
Reservations: 903 665 8616/665 8617

Innkeepers:	Steve & Nonie Turner, Resident Owners
Open:	All Year
Facilities:	4 Bedrooms, All Private Baths
Breakfast:	Continental Plus
Rates:	$70 - $80 For 2 Guests
Payment:	All Major, Check

TWIN OAKS COUNTRY INN

Hwy 134 South
Jefferson 75657
Reservations: 903 665 3535

Innkeepers:	Carol & Vernon Randale
	Resident Owners
Open:	All Year
Facilities:	5 Bedrooms, All Private Baths
	Plus 1Bed-1bath Bungalow
Breakfast:	Full
Rates:	$95 - $100 For 2 Guests
Payment:	All Major,Check

URQUHART HOUSE OF ELEVEN GABLES

301 East Walker Street
Jefferson 75657
Reservations: 903 665 8442

Innkeeper:	Joyce Jackson, Resident Owner
Open:	All Year
Facilities:	1 Suite With Pvt Bath
Breakfast:	Full
Rates:	$75 - $115 Fo4 2 Guests
Payment:	Check

WISE MANOR

312 Houston St
Jefferson 75657
Reservations: 903 665 2386

Innkeeper:	Katherine Wise, Resident Owner
Open:	All Year
Facilities:	3 Bedrooms, All Private Baths
Breakfast:	Full
Rates:	$55 For 2 Guests
Payment:	MC,Visa,Check

Johnson City

A ROOM WITH A VIEW

Ranch Rd 3232, RR1, Box 381
Johnson City 78636
Reservations: 210 868 7668

Innkeeper:	Ann Passino, Owner
Open:	All Year
Facilities:	4 Bedrooms, All Private Baths
Breakfast:	Gourmet
Rates:	$75 - $90 For 2 Guests
Payment:	Check

DREAM CATCHER BED & BREAKFAST

County Rt. 214 Off RR 3232
Johnson City 78636
Reservations: 210 868 4875

Innkeepers:	Lee & Peggy Arbon
	Resident Owners
Open:	All Year
Facilities:	1 Bunkhouse, 2 Sleeping Tepees
Breakfast:	Continental-See Note
Rates:	$60 - $85 For 2 Guests
Payment:	Check

Nestled among 20 rural acres in the fabled Texas Hill country, Dream Catcher Bed and Breakfast is quite literally in the "boonies" where the atmosphere is serene, quiet and restful and it's 15 miles to anything!! Your hosts, Lee and Peggy Arbon, had a dream . . . and Dream Catcher Bed & Breakfast is that dream come true. They became spellbound with a beautiful tepee that they viewed on TV, and started to dream of having their own. They came up with a way to realize that dream. Six months later they had their own tepee, and had restored their old (not too old) cabin into a bunkhouse for a "Cowboys and Indians" theme. Hence the name "Dream Catcher".

Born-again Bunkhouse is that restored cabin, boasting 600 sq.ft. of space, located beneath a magnificent elm tree. It has been tastefully decorated in a western motif with simple, comfortable furnishings and a private bathroom. Luxurious down pillows, comforters and cotton line-dried bed linens are provided.

Dream Catcher Tipis are for the more outdoor oriented. Sioux tipis are pitched in a stand of large oaks about 100 yards from the host's residence and in the opposite direction from the bunkhouse. The carpeted tipis sleep three to five comfortably on raised futons. Electricity and running water is provided, along with toilet facilities (the "pipi tipi") but no bath. Camping in a Dream Catcher Tipi is truly a unique and exciting experience.

The Arbons (in their 70's and enjoying their avocation) serve a "Luck-of-the-Draw" breakfast which can be anything from Continental to Full. Snacks and drinks are also provided.

Non-smoking facility. Children are welcome. Reservations are required.

Member: Texas Hotel/Motel Association

 # Karnack

THE SUMMERS HOUSE BED & BREAKFAST
Rt. 2, Box 100D, Pine Island Rd
Karnack 75661
Reservations: 903 679 4364

Innkeepers:	Herb & Faye Summers
	Residednt Owners
Open:	All Year
Facilities:	2 Bedroom, 1.5 Bath Cottage
Breakfast:	Continental
Rates:	$85 For 2 Guests
Payment:	Check

TIMBERWILD FARM
1 Mi. West Of Caddo Lake St Pk
Karnack 75661
Reservations: 903 679 3326

Innkeepers:	Richard & Sarah Leander
	Resident Owners
Open:	All Year
Facilities:	1 Bedroom, 1 Bath Guest Cottage
Breakfast:	Continental Plus
Rates:	$85 For 2 Guests
Payment:	MC,Visa,Check

 # Kemah

THE CAPTAIN'S QUARTERS
701 Bay Avenue
Kemah 77565
Reservations: 713 334 4141

Innkeepers:	Mary & Royston Patterson
	Resident Owners
Open:	All Year
Facilities:	5 Bedrooms, All Private Baths
Breakfast:	Full
Rates:	$55 - $120 For 2 Guests
Payment:	Amex,Check

 # Kerrville

KERRVILLE'S BED & BREAKFAST
2873 Bandera Hwy
Kerrville 78028
Reservations: 210 257 8750

Innkeeper:	Charles Dunlap, Resident Owner
Open:	All Year
Facilities:	2 Bedrooms, 1 Bath
Breakfast:	Continental Plus
Rates:	$50 For 2 Guests
Payment:	MC,Visa,Check

LA REATA RANCH BED & BREAKFAST
2555 Sheppard-Rees Rd
Kerrville 78028
Reservations: 210 896 5503

Innkeepers:	Goerge & Florence Schulgen
	Resident Owners
Open:	All Year
Facilities:	Two 2 Bedroom - 2 Bath
	Guest Cottages
Breakfast:	Continental Plus
Rates:	$65 - $85 For 2 Guests
Payment:	All Major,Check

NOPALITOS HIDEAWAY
7001 Medina Hwy
Kerrville 78028
Reservations: 210 257 7815

Innkeepers:	Rodney & Michele Traeger
	Resident Owner
Open:	All Year
Facilities:	2 Bedroom, 1 Bath House
Breakfast:	OYO
Rates:	$135 For 2 Guests
Payment:	Check

KERRVILLE

The county seat for Kerr County, Kerrville is an area that many believe to have the most ideal climate in the country. At an altitude of 1,645 feet, amidst hills covered by live oak and cedar, picturesque green valleys and idyllic streams edged by towering cypress would delight any traveler. White-trailed deer are so plentiful that motorists are cautioned to be on the alert for them, especially at night.

One of the state's most popular health and recreation areas, Kerrville has more than two dozen boys' and girls' camps, dude ranches, museums, religious encampments and scores of accommodations. Some of the major annual events are the Experimental Aircraft Association Fly-In and Air Show in October and the Texas State Arts and Crafts Fair on Memorial Day weekend.

There is a fascinating old section of town which now houses art studios, galleries, antique shops, boutiques and restaurants you won't want to miss. Music festivals featuring folk and country western stars are usually held on Memorial Day and Labor day weekends.

The Texas Heritage Music Museum contains memorabilia of Texas musicians and features performances of local writers and musicians. There is also the Cowboy Artists of America Museum featuring permanent and rotating collections and workshops by artists in residence and the Hill Country Museum with its local artifacts, antiques and memorabilia located in the home of Captain Charles A. Schreiner, a prominent citizen in the 1860's.

Kingsville

B BAR B RANCH INN

RR#1, Box 457
Kingsville 78363
Reservations: 512 296 3331/512 850 6537

Innkeepers:	Luther & Patti Young
	Resident Owners
Open:	All Year
Facilities:	7 Bedrooms
	5 Private Baths, 1 Shared
Breakfast:	Gourmet
Rates:	$75 - $100 For 2 Guests
Payment:	Check

Quietly nestled beneath the rippling leaves of a South Texas mesquite grove, the B Bar B Ranch Inn offers a unique retreat for business or pleasure. Originally part of the historic King Ranch, the Inn retains the rustic look and feel of the Old West. However, the ranch has been completely restored to a splendid lodge with all the modern conveniences.

Surrounded by a 220 acre working ranch, the B Bar B is host to a wide variety of native plants and wildlife. The fresh air and gentle winds provide the ideal environment for bird-watching (there are two Great Horned Owls living at their pond), picnicking or other outdoor activities. A fresh water pond and nearby Baffin Bay also provide excellent year-round fishing.

For those who wish to enjoy the area, you might tour the legendary King Ranch (free with a two night stay) or visit the Henrietta King Memorial, Connor Museum and the historic Ragland Building or and it's only 90 minutes to Mexico to enjoy the shopping, dining and culture of Matamoros. Golfers can enjoy a game at a course just minutes away.

Breakfast is served in the dining room, on the patio or in the privacy of your own room. Snacks and beverages are provided. Lunch and dinner can be arranged at an additional cost.

Amenities at B BAR B include two hot tubs, a swimming pool, gazebo/picnic area, telephones, satellite TV, laundry facilities and pet kennels.

Smoking must be done in the great outdoors. The Inn accommodates children over twelve. Reservations are required. Rates for senior citizens.

Directions: Hwy 77 South of Kingsville. Go eight miles and turn Left at B Bar B sign - travel East to end of road.

Member: Professional Assn of Innkeepers Int'l. and Texas Hotel/Motel Association

 **La Coste**

SWAN & RAILWAY COUNTRY INN
BED & BREAKFAST

11280 Castro Ave
La Coste 78039
Reservations: 210 762 3742

Innkeepers:	Jaye & Gene Sherrer
	Resident Owners
Open:	All Year
Facilities:	7 Bedrooms
	4 Private Baths, 1 Shared
Breakfast:	Full
Rates:	$60 - $75 For 2 Guests
Payment:	Check

198

Built in 1912, The Swan & Railway Country Inn is a small, historical hotel, originally named "City Hotel". It was the first hotel built West of San Antonio to serve the Southern Pacific Railroad. It is situated next to the railroad tracks in the downtown area of La Coste. There's a Texas State Historical Marker!

The old hotel has been beautifully restored, furnished in lovely antiques and offers the very best in bed and breakfast lodging. Relax, rest, rejuvenate and just enjoy the charm of an old world atmosphere. All rooms are located in the upstairs area with a French door in each bedroom entering the porch area where guests may sit in private while train-watching or visit with other guests. A back stairway leads down to a large, beautiful swimming pool.

Some of the rooms have private baths, and some shared baths. Each room has one double or Queen bed per room. The baths have antique claw foot tubs with a brass ring around the top and porcelain shower heads, ideal for relaxing bubble baths or fresh showers.

Delicious breakfasts are served in the large living-dining area with a cozy fireplace or in the Garden Tea Room where guests sometimes gather to play cards, dominoes or have a friendly visit with hosts, Eugene & Jaye Sherrer. Afternoon tea is served, and snacks and beverages are provided.

House Rules are No Pets, No Smoking, No Children and No Credit Cards. Cash, travelers checks or good personal checks are appreciated. Reservations are required.

Directions: From San Antonio city limit sign, take Hwy 90 West about 7 miles, look for La Coste sign at Bippert Lane, then Left to La Coste (three miles South of Hwy. 90)

La Grange

BLUE CABOOSE BED AND BREAKFAST

311 N. Washington
La Grange 78945
Reservations: 409 968 5053/800 968 5053

Innkeeper:	K. J. Bergstrom
Open:	All Year
Facilities:	2 Bedrooms, All Private Baths
Breakfast:	Full
Rates:	$45 - $65 For 2 Guests
Payment:	MC,Visa,Check

Y KNOT BED & BREAKFAST

2819 Frank Road
La Grange 78945
Reservations: 409 247 4529

Innkeeper:	Peggy Edwards, Resident Owner
Open:	All Year
Facilities:	2 Bedrooms, All Private Baths
Breakfast:	Continental Plus
Rates:	$65 For 2 Guests
Payment:	Visa,Check

The Bed & Breakfast Association
of Fayette County - Texas

From rustic to elegant, each bed and breakfast and guest cottage has its own distinct personality. Located "Off the Beaten Path", yet within easy driving distance of Houston, Dallas/Fort Worth, San Antonio, Austin and Corpus Christi, there are over 20 lodging accommodations in Fayette County, nestled in rural settings near or in the communities of Carmine, Fayetteville, Ledbetter, LaGrange, Round Top, Schulenburg and Warrenton.

As guests travel the area, they may wish to visit and shop the 1890's Town Squares, tour Early Texas restorations and museums, view historic sites and monuments, unique courthouses and churches, general stores and "saloons". They may experience the Czech/German heritage and culture, enjoy concerts and theater, festivals and fairs, and in all communities - antique/collectible shops and shows.

Of special interest are spectacular April bluebonnet trails, Monument Hill/Kreische Brewery State Park, the 1890's Fayette County Courthouse and Square at LaGrange, Schulenburg's famous "Painted Churches" tour, Festival Hill, Winedale and Henkel Square at Round Top, a Picnic Park at Carmine, the 110 year old General Store and the Buggy Shop at Ledbetter, the "World's Smallest Church" at Warrenton, and the 1880's Town Square with courthouse, bandstand and false-front buildings in the tiny town of Fayetteville.

For Further Information please contact
Bed & Breakfast Association of Fayette County
419 S. Main Street
LaGrange, Texas 78945
Telephone: (409) 968-8787

MEERSCHEIDT HAUS
(LA GRANGE B&B)

458 N. Monroe Street
La Grange 78945
Reservations: 409 968 9569

Innkeepers:	Elva & Royce Keilers
	Owners/Managers
Open:	All Year
Facilities:	4 Bedrooms, All Private Baths
Breakfast:	Continental Plus
Rates:	$45 - $85 For 2 Guests
Payment:	MC,Visa,Check

Built in the early 1880's by Axel Meerscheidt, this Victorian home has seen a procession of prominent citizens in residence. Located on historic Block Number One, the property once housed the public water well for the city as well as the public livery stable. Innkeepers Elva and Royce Keilers have restored the home and furnished it with period antiques for your enjoyment.

Downstairs guests enjoy the elegantly appointed Rose Room with Queen size bed and the cheerful Sun room with matching antique double beds, each with a charming private bath. Upstairs the Country Suite consists of two special bedrooms, two baths and an inviting conversation area. The Rafters with Queen size bed and The Eaves with ornate day bed and trundle, may be used as a living area or as a comfortable second bedroom for additional persons. The suite can also be made available as two individual bedrooms with private baths.

Your Continental Plus breakfast is served in the formal dining room at your leisure and includes fresh German/Czech kolaches and pigs-in-blankets, homebaked breads and local jams and jellies, healthy homemade granola, seasonal fruit and juices. Afternoon Tea, snacks and beverages are also provided for guests.

This is a non-smoking facility. Children over twelve can be accommodated. Pets must be in a carrier or kept outdoors. Handicap accessible with assistance only. Reservations are required. Corporate rates offered weekdays. A discount is given to guests utilizing hospital facilities.

Member: Pioneer Trail, Texas Hotel/Motel Assn, Historic Home Assn of Texas

Lampasas

HISTORIC MOSES HUGHES RANCH
BED & BREAKFAST

On 580 West, 7 Mi. From Town
Lampasas 76550
Reservations: 512 556 5923

Innkeepers: Al & Beverly Solomon
Resident Owners
Open: All Year
Facilities: 2 Bedrooms , All Private Baths
Breakfast: Gourmet
Rates: $75 - $85 For 2 Guests
Payment: Check

A "must stay" for anyone traveling Lampasas way, the Historic Moses Hughes Ranch Bed & Breakfast was built in 1856 by the first white settler and founder of this friendly town. The Hughes family was drawn to the area after hearing stories from American Indians about the area's healthful springs.

Situated on 40 beautiful acres with a spring-fed creek, this homesite has been an official Texas Wildscape since 1994. Your hosts, Al and Beverly Solomon, formerly Houston area residents, have created a home-away-from-home for travelers, accentuated by their extensive collection of native American artifacts and Texana. The Solomons are knowledgeable about local wildlife, historic sites and area shopping.

Two upstairs bedrooms, the Oak Room and the Quilt Room, are warm and inviting to guests. Both rooms open onto a splendid wooden balcony where guests can enjoy the view. There are gathering places in the kitchen, living room and dining room .

A gourmet breakfast is served in the dining room and afternoon tea, snacks and beverages are offered. On occasion, complimentary wine is available to guests.

Accommodations are by reservation only. This is a non-smoking facility. There are no provisions for children or pets. There is a two night minimum stay on weekends and holidays.

Directions: Seven miles West on FM 580 going toward Colorado Bend State Park from Lampasas.
Member: American Assn of Historic Inns (Texas Historic Landmark since I966)

 **Lakehills**

WANDERING AENGUS COTTAGE
Geronimo Springs Dr, Rt 4, Box 4725
Lakehills 78063
Reservations: 210 751 3345

Innkeepers:	Gail & Gary Lane, Resident Owners
Open:	All Year
Facilities:	5 Room Cottage With Bath
Breakfast:	OYO
Rates:	$84 For 2 Guests
Payment:	MC,Visa,Check

 **Leakey**

JOLLY CREEK CABIN
Hwy 83, 2 Mi South Of Leakey
Leakey 78873
Reservations: 210 966 2320

Innkeepers:	Leann & Anthony Sharp, Managers
Open:	All Year
Facilities:	2 Bedroom Cabin With Bath
Breakfast:	OYO
Rates:	$70 For 2 Guests
Payment:	Check

LEAKEY HOMESTEAD
Old Main Street
Leakey 78873
Reservations: 210 966 2320

Innkeepers:	Leann & Anthony Sharp, Managers
Open:	All Year
Facilities:	1 Bedroom Home With Bath
Breakfast:	OYO
Rates:	$85 For 2 Guests
Payment:	Check

RIO LINDO CABIN
Off RR #336, 2 Mi North Of Leakey
Leakey 78873
Reservations: 210 966 2320

Innkeepers:	Leann & Anthony Sharp, Managers
Open:	All Year
Facilities:	2 Bedroom Cabin With Bath
Breakfast:	OYO
Rates:	$100 For 2 Guests
Payment:	Check

WHISKEY MOUNTAIN INN
HCR 1, Box 555
Leakey 78873
Reservations: 210 232 6797/800 370 6797

Innkeepers:	Darrell & Judy Adams
	Resident Owners
Open:	All Year
Facilities:	2 Bedrooms, All Private Baths
Breakfast:	Continental Plus
Rates:	$55 For 2 Guests
Payment:	MC, Visa,Check

 **Ledbetter**

GRANNY'S HOUSE BED & BREAKFAST
F.M. 1291 & Congress
Ledbetter 78946
Reservations: 409 249 3066

Innkeepers:	Chris & Jay Jervis, Resident Owners
Open:	All Year
Facilities:	4 Bedrooms, All Private Baths
Breakfast:	Full
Rates:	$70 For 2 Guests
Payment:	MC,Visa,Check

LEDBETTER HOTEL BED & BREAKFAST
Hwy 290 & F.M. 1291
Ledbetter 78946
Reservations: 409 249 3066

Innkeepers:	Chris & Jay Jervis, Owners
Open:	All Year
Facilities:	3 Bedrooms, All Private Baths
Breakfast:	Full
Rates:	$70 For 2 Guests
Payment:	MC,Visa,Check

MOTHERS ANNEX BED & BREAKFAST
Brenham Streeet
Ledbetter 78946
Reservations: 409 249 3066

Innkeepers:	Chris & Jay Jervis, Managers
Open:	All Year
Facilities:	1 Bedroom With Bath
Breakfast:	Full
Rates:	$70 For 2 Guests
Payment:	MC,Visa,Check

STORK HOUSE BED & BREAKFAST

F.M. 1291 & Brenham St
Ledbetter 78946
Reservations: 409 249 3066

Innkeepers:	Chris & Jay Jervis, Resident Owners
Open:	All Year
Facilities:	4 Bedrooms, All Private Baths
Breakfast:	Full
Rates:	$70 For 2 Guests
Payment:	MC,Visa,Check

STUERMER HOUSE BED & BREAKFAST

F.M. 1291 & Congress
Ledbetter 78946
Reservations: 409 249 3066

Innkeepers:	Chris & Jay Jervis, Resident Owners
Open:	All Year
Facilities:	4 Bedrooms, 2 Pvt Baths, 1 Shared
Breakfast:	Full
Rates:	$70 For 2 Guests
Payment:	MC,Visa,Check

VANDERWERTH HOUSE BED & BREAKFAST

Congress & Ledbetter Dell
Ledbetter 78946
Reservations: 409 249 3066

Innkeepers:	Chris & Jay Jervis, Managers
Open:	All Year
Facilities:	3 Bedroom, 1 Pvt Bath, 1 Shared
Breakfast:	Full
Rates:	$70 For 2 Guests
Payment:	MC,Visa,Check

 # Linn

SANTILLANA RANCH OF SOUTH TEXAS
7 Mi. West Of Hwy 281 On 1017
Linn 78563
Reservations: 210 380 0111

Innkeeper:	Melissa Guerra, Manager
Open:	All Year
Facilities:	3 Bedrooms, 1 Pvt Bath, 1 Shared Plus 4 Bed-4 Bath Lodge
Breakfast:	Incl All Meals
Rates:	$187.50 For 2 Guests
Payment:	Check

 # Longview

FISHER FARM BED & BREAKFAST
Country Club Road
Longview 75602
Reservations: 903 660 2978

Innkeepers:	John & Jan Fisher
Open:	All Year
Facilities:	4 Bedrooms, All Private Baths
Breakfast:	Full
Rates:	$99 For 2 Guests
Payment:	MC, Visa,Check

 **Lubbock**

BROADWAY MANOR BED & BREAKFAST
1811 Broadway
Lubbock 79401
Reservations: 806 749 4707

Innkeeper:	Randy Wright, Owner
Open:	All Year
Facilities:	5 Bedrooms, 2 Pvt Baths, 1 Shared
Breakfast:	Continental Plus
Rates:	$65 - $85 For 2 Guests
Payment:	MC, Visa,Check

CONTINENTAL BED & BREAKFAST
2224 Broadway
Lubbock 79401
Reservations: 806 762 3377

Innkeepers:	Tom & Mandy Wiley, Resident Owners
Open:	All Year
Facilities:	2 Bedrooms, All Private Baths
Breakfast:	Gourmet
Rates:	$75 For 2 Guests
Payment:	All Major, Check

WOODROW HOUSE
2629 19th Street
Lubbock 79410
Reservations: 806 749 3330

Innkeepers:	David & Dawn Fleming, Res.Owners
Open:	All Year
Facilities:	5 Bedrooms, All Private Baths
Breakfast:	Full
Rates:	$75 For 2 Guests
Payment:	MC,Visa,Amex,Chec

 **Marfa**

THE LASH-UP BED & BREAKFAST
215 N. Austin
Marfa 79843
Reservations: 915 749 4487

Innkeeper:	Lillian Parker, Resident Owner
Open:	All Year
Facilities:	3 Bedrooms, 1 Pvt Bath, 1 Shared
Breakfast:	Full
Rates:	$50 - $55 For 2 Guests
Payment:	MC,Visa,Check

Marshall

MANDALAY BED & BREAKFAST
1107 South Washington
Marshall 75670
Reservations: 903 938 8860

Innkeeper:	Frank McCracken, Resident Owner
Open:	All Year
Facilities:	2 Suites, 1 Bedroom, All Private Baths
Breakfast:	Gourmet
Rates:	$75 - $110 For 2 Guests
Payment:	Check

SCOTT-JOHNSON PLANTATION

Highway 80 East
Marshall 75670
Reservations: 903 935 7579

Innkeepers:	Jimmy & Gerry Johnson
	Resident Owners
Open:	All Year
Facilities:	2 Bedrooms, All Private Baths
Breakfast:	Full
Rates:	$80 For 2 Guests
Payment:	MC,Visa,Check

WOOD BOONE NORRELL HOUSE
BED AND BREAKFAST

215 E. Rusk St
Marshall 75670
Reservations: 903 935 1800/800 423 1356

Innkeepers:	Mike & Patsy Norrell, Resident Owners
Open:	All Year
Facilities:	5 Bedrooms, All Private Baths
Breakfast:	Full
Rates:	$75 - $80 For 2 Guests
Payment:	MC,Visa,Amex,Check

HISTORY HOUSE FOR GUESTS

308 West Houston
Marshall 75670
Reservations: 903 938 9171

Innkeeper:	Anne Dennis, Owner
Open:	All Year
Facilities:	2 Bedroom, 1 Bath Guest House
Breakfast:	Continental Plus OYO
Rates:	$45 For 1 Guest, $10 Each Addl
Payment:	MC,Visa,Check

Going through downtown Marshall, you won't find a guest house sign in front of History House for Guests. This attractively preserved 1917 Prairie-style house has a second-floor guest house nestled among the trees just one block from the historic square. With a relaxed, homey atmosphere, History House invites individuals, couples or families to stay a night, a weekend or more to enjoy small-town living at its best.

The guest house is tastefully decorated with comfortable hand-crafted furniture and an array of historic photographs, drawings, artifacts and artworks that speak of Marshall's unique past.

This accommodation sleeps six in two bedrooms (King bed, two single beds) and on a Queen sleeper sofa in the living room. The large bath has a tub with shower, and there is a dining room and laundry room for your use. Guests are welcome to sit on the tree-shaded balcony and watch the world go by. Books, games, toys, cable TV and a VCR are also available to make your stay more enjoyable.

Hostess Anne Dennis keeps the refrigerator stocked with the makings for light breakfasts and snacks.

No smoking or alcohol consumption on the premises. Well-behaved, well-supervised children are welcome but no pets, please! Reservations are required. Ample off-street parking is available. Plan to check in before 5 p.m. and check out before 12 noon.

Directions: From US Hwy 59 (East End Blvd) turn West onto E. Houston Street; follow Houston St. around the town square and continue West for two more blocks to #308.

THREE OAKS BED & BREAKFAST

609 North Washington
Marshall 75670
Reservations: 903 935 6777

Innkeepers:	Tony & Laurie Overhultz
	Resident Owners
Open:	All Year
Facilities:	4 Bedrooms, All Private Baths
Breakfast:	Gourmet & Continental
Rates:	$65 - $95 For 2 Guests
Payment:	MC,Visa,Check

216

An 1895 Victorian home listed in the National Register of Historic Places, Three Oaks Bed & Breakfast is located in the Ginocchio Historic District of Marshall. The magnificent 13 room structure highlights original leaded glass transoms, seven hand carved fireplaces, egg and dart trim, beamed ceilings, cut glass French doors and polished oak flooring and an antique piano and pump organ which guests may play.

This romantic home, completely restored, has The Victorian Room (also known as the Honeymoon Suite) has a fireplace and gourmet snack tray provided for guests, a King size iron bed, sitting area and an antique claw foot tub and shower in your private bath. The Magnolia Room has a double bed with private bath, claw foot tub in the sunroom, and a cheerful sitting area with wicker and plants. The Eastlake Room invites sweet dreams with a solid cherry bedroom suite which has a massive headboard over six feet tall. In the Ginocchio Room an antique King size bed will lure you off to sleep, but you won't need the provided chamber pot with your private bath including a claw foot tub.

A Continental Plus breakfast is served Monday - Friday and full gourmet fare is offered on Saturday and Sunday. Afternoon refreshments are served on the porch under the three surviving Burr Oaks grown from acorns brought from the "Old Country". Other meal arrangements upon request.

Smoking on outside veranda only. Children are welcome. Pets cannot be accommodated. Reservations are required. Weekday corporate discounts.

Directions: West on Hwy 80 to right on N. Washington. Second block on left .

 **Mason**

HASSE HOUSE & RANCH

P.O. Box 58
Mason 76856
Reservations: 915 347 6463

Innkeeper:	Laverne Lee, Resident Owner
Open:	All Year
Facilities:	2 Bedrooms, 2 Private Baths
Breakfast:	Continental OYO
Rates:	$85 For 2 Guests
Payment:	MC,Visa,Check

Avoid the routes frequented by others and travel seven miles East of Mason to Art, Texas, where you will discover the historic 1883 German salt box Hasse House & Ranch located on 320 acres where deer, wild turkey, feral hogs and quail are common sights. The two mile hiking path will give guests the quiet feeling of country life and tranquillity in the midst of the rare beauty of the Texas Hill Country. Guests might try a little Topaz (a diamond-like gem found only in Mason County in Texas) hunting for fun.

Hostess Laverne Lee, a fourth generation Hasse, will welcome you and mention with pride that the Hasse House is listed in the National Register of Historic Places, has been awarded a Certificate of Honor by the Texas Department of Agriculture and featured on various television programs. Her obvious love of this home is reflected in the details of its restoration and her willingness to share her heritage with guests.

The guest house is reserved for only one party and comes complete with period furniture and a wood-burning stove as well as a full kitchen with microwave and dishwasher, two bedrooms, two baths, living /dining area and washer/dryer.

Your hostess will leave breakfast fixin's in the refrigerator for you to prepare at your leisure.

Smoking is permitted and children are welcome. Pets, however, cannot be accommodated. The house is handicap accessible. Reservations are required. Extended stay discounts are offered. Tennis and golf available at nearby facilities.

Directions: Six miles East of Mason on Texas Highway 29.

HOMESTEAD BED & BREAKFAST
South 1Mi. On 1723
Mason 76856
Reservations: 915 347 6816

Innkeeper:	Joann Wilson, Resident Owner
Open:	All Year
Facilities:	1 Bedroom With Bath
Breakfast:	Full
Rates:	$65 For 2 Guests
Payment:	Check

HUMMING BIRD B&B
Highway 87 South
Mason 76856
Reservations: 915 347 6982/347 5249

Innkeeper:	Jeff Grote, Resident Owner
Open:	All Year
Facilities:	1 Bedroom With Bath
Breakfast:	Continental Plus
Rates:	$45 For 2 Guests
Payment:	Inquire

MASON SQUARE BED & BREAKFAST
134 Ft. McKavitt
Mason 76856
Reservations: 915 347 6398/800 369 0405

Innkeepers:	Monica & Brent Hinckley, Owners
Open:	All Year
Facilities:	3 Bedrooms, All Private Baths
Breakfast:	Continental Plus
Rates:	$40 - $60 For 2 Guests
Payment:	Check

 # McGregor

LIGHTHOUSE BED & BREAKFAST

421 S. Harrison
McGregor 76657
Reservations: 817 840 2683/800 840 2683

Innkeepers:	Jerry & Jan Walters, Resident Owners
Open:	All Year
Facilities:	8 Bedrooms, 6.5 Pvt Baths, 2 Shared
Breakfast:	Full
Rates:	$50 - $60 For 2 Guests
Payment:	All Major, Check

 # Memphis

MEMPHIS HOTEL BED & BREAKFAST

108 North 5th St.
Memphis 79245
Reservations: 806 259 2198

Innkeepers:	The Hall Family, Resident Owners
Open:	All Year
Facilities:	11 Bedrooms, All Private Baths
Breakfast:	Full
Rates:	$40 For 2 Guests
Payment:	Check

 # Meridian

HASTINGS HOUSE BED & BREAKFAST
13 Mi. West Of Town
Meridian 76665
Reservations: 817 597 2761

Innkeeper:	Mary Hastings, Resident Owner
Open:	All Year
Facilities:	3 Bedroom, 1 Bath House
Breakfast:	OYO
Rates:	$65 - $95 For 2 Guests
Payment:	Check

 # Miami

HOWERTON HOUSE BED & BREAKFAST
P.O. Box 222
Miami 79059
Reservations: 806 868 4771

Innkeepers:	Peggy & Dannia Howerton Resident Owners
Open:	All Year
Facilities:	12 Bedrooms, 5 Pvt Baths, 1.5 Shared
Breakfast:	Gourmet
Rates:	$45 - $60 For 2 Guests
Payment:	MC,Visa,Check

 **Mineola**

FALL FARM BED & BREAKFAST
8 Mi. North Of Town
Mineola 75773
Reservations: 903 768 2449

Innkeepers:	Mike & Carole Fall, Resident Owners
Open:	All Year
Facilities:	8 Bedrooms, 3 Pvt Baths, 1 Shared
Breakfast:	Continental Plus
Rates:	$65 - $95 For 2 Guests
Payment:	MC,Visa,Check

MINEOLA -

Railroadman Ira H. Evans named the town for his daughter, Ola, and her friend, Minnie !

MUNZESHEIMER MANOR

202 N. Newsom
Mineola 75773
Reservations: 903 569 6634

Innkeepers:	Bob & Sherry Murray
	Resident Owners
Open:	All Year
Facilities:	7 Bedrooms, All Private Baths
Breakfast:	Gourmet
Rates:	$75 - $95 For 2 Guests
Payment:	Most Major,Check

Totally restored to its former elegance, this 1898 two story Princess Anne Victorian home with wrap-around porches, sitting on a tree-filled corner lot, captures the charm of days gone by. . . and time seems to stand still at Munzesheimer Manor. The gardens, pathways and park benches provide an ideal getaway from the busy buzz of everyday life. Be sure to see the secret "drinking room" which was uncovered during the restoration of this 4,000 square foot home.

Built of pine and cedar by a German immigrant for his bride, there is a formal dining room, two parlors and seven fireplaces (three in guest rooms). Furnished in American and English antiques, all guest rooms have private baths with period footed tubs.

The Murray's have added their own special touches to your stay such as Victorian gowns and sleepshirts for your use, non-alcoholic cider on your arrival, custom soaps and fresh flowers. You'll see rockers rocking on the porches in Spring, Summer and Fall and in Winter visitors enjoy flames flickering in the fireplaces.

Custom blended coffee is delivered just outside your room an hour before breakfast (what luxury!) and a gourmet breakfast is served in the formal dining room on crystal, china and silver. Picnic lunches are available with advance notice.

Smoking is limited to the porches and gardens. The inn can accommodate children who sleep all night, and it is wheelchair accessible. There are no provisions for pets.   Reservations are advisable. Weekday business rates are offered.

Member: Professional Assn of Innkeepers Int'l, Texas Hotel/Motel Assn, B&B's of East Texas

NOBLE MANOR

411 E. Kilpatrick
Mineola 75773
Reservations: 903 569 5720

Innkeepers:	Rick & Shirley Gordon
	Resident Owners
Open:	All Year
Facilities:	9 Bedrooms, All Private Baths
Breakfast:	Full
Rates:	$80 - $125 For 2 Guests
Payment:	MC,Visa,Amex,Check

Built for the Noble family in 1910, this stately 19 room Greek Revival mansion was constructed of lumber cut and milled in Wood County. The original hardwood floors have been restored and gleam beneath needlepoint rugs among antique furnishings. Vintage chandeliers illuminate the spacious dining and living rooms, each with fireplaces, as well as the grand entrance hall and various commons areas.

Each individual and spacious suite enjoys a private bath and individual coffee service and reflects the history of the home. There is even a "Cupid's Cottage" nestled among the trees a few steps from the main house for lovers of all ages. Once a servant's quarters, the refurbished little house features stained glass windows, his and her claw foot tubs and an Queen size hand-carved cherub sleighbed from the 1800's.

Guests choose between a full breakfast and sparkling conversation in Noble Manor's spacious dining area or a more secluded table to relish hot coffee and intimate conversation.

For the safety and consideration of others, smoking is only permitted outdoors. Children are welcome. Pets cannot be accommodated. A hot tub is on site for your use. Tennis and golf are available at nearby facilities. Check in is between 3-9 p.m. and check out is 11 a.m. Rates are for single/double occupancy and additional guests in room are charged $15 per night.

Directions: 80 miles East of Dallas on Hwy 80. 24 miles North of Tyler on Hwy 69. Kilpatrick St. is 1 block North of Hwy 69/80 intersection. Go East on Kilpatrick 3 blocks.

Member: Professional Assn of Innkeepers Int'l, Bed & Breakfast Direct

 # Moody

LITTLE COUNTRY INN BED & BREAKFAST
1347 Winchester
Moody 76524
Reservations: 817 853 2498

Innkeepers:	Anita & Richard Eberspacher
	Resident Owners
Open:	All Year
Facilities:	Four Bedrooms, 1 Pvt Bath, 1 Shared
Breakfast:	Full
Rates:	$60 For 2 Guests
Payment:	Check

 # Mt. Pleasant

TANKERSLEY GARDENS
Tankersley Rd At Loop 221/I-30 W
Mt. Pleasant 75455
Reservations: 903 572 0567

Innkeepers:	Jim & Narlene Capel, Resident Owners
Open:	All Year
Facilities:	2 Bedrooms, 1 Bath Pvt Or Shared
Breakfast:	Gourmet Or OYO
Rates:	$45 - $110 For 2 Guests
Payment:	Check

# Mt. Vernon

MISS IKIE'S BED & BREAKFAST

110 Oak Street
Mt. Vernon 75457
Reservations: 903 537 7002

Innkeepers:	Ikie & Bob Richards, Resident Owners
Open:	All Year
Facilities:	7 Bedrooms, 2 Pvt Baths, 2 Shared
Breakfast:	Full
Rates:	$65 - $75 For 2 Guests
Payment:	MC,Visa,Check

# Nacogdoches

LLANO GRANDE PLANTATION B&B

Route 4, Box 9400
Nacogdoches 75964
Reservations: 409 569 1249

Innkeepers:	Capt. Charles & Ann Phillips Resident Owners
Open:	All Year
Facilities:	Three 2 Bed - 1 Bath Houses
Breakfast:	Full
Rates:	$60 - $70 For 2 Guests
Payment:	Check

ANDERSON POINT BED & BREAKFAST

29 East Lake Estates
Nacogdoches 75964
Reservations: 409 569 7445

Innkeepers: Ron & Rachel Anderson
    Resident Owner
Open: All Year
Facilities: 2 Bedrooms, Shared Bath
Breakfast: Continental Plus
Rates: $50 - $60 For 2 Guests
Payment: Check

View beautiful Lake Nacogdoches from every room in this lovely two story, French-style home surrounded by 300 feet of lake frontage. You won't want to leave Anderson Point Bed & Breakfast! Your hosts, Ron and Rachel Anderson, utilize the upstairs, but the downstairs is all yours to enjoy.

Guests are invited to stroll the beautiful grounds, swim or fish off the pier. The home and grounds are unique in that no toxic chemicals or fragrances are used (no smoking is allowed). The most severe allergy sufferers will be safe in this pristine environment. The healthy minded may round out their stay with a visit to the exercise room featuring a nautilus machine, exercise bike, treadmill, trampoline and sauna.

The spacious King's Room offers a King size bed with two six-foot sliding doors to bring the outside in as you fall asleep listening to the waves lap on the shore. The cozy Queen's Room will delight the heart of the antique buff. Filled with family heirlooms it provides a Queen size bed.

A Continental Plus breakfast pantry is provided every morning. Guests may choose to eat in the Sitting Room with its wide selection of books, a fireplace and wet bar or dine out on the veranda.

The bed and breakfast does not have facilities to accommodate children. Inquire regarding pets. Check in time is 4 p.m. and check out is at 11 a.m.

Directions: FM 225 to Alazan, turn Right on East Lake Road 751, Enter East Lake Estates, stay to Left, dead-end of road. (20 minutes from Nacogdoches)

EAGLE'S AERIE

12 East Lake Estates
Nacogdoches 75964
Reservations: 409 564 7995

Innkeeper: Rod Allen, Resident Owner
Open: All Year
Facilities: 2 Bedroom, 1 Bath In Log House
Breakfast: OYO
Rates: $50 For 2 Guests
Payment: MC,Visa,Check

**_Special_: Mention this book when making your
reservation and receive a special treat**

Eagle's Aerie offers guests their own apartment in a log house with 2,210 acre Lake Nacogdoches right outside your door. Sit in your own living room and contemplate nature at its finest. Guests who feel more energetic can take a swim, hike along a nearby marked nature trail, or skim along in a canoe with fingers trailing the water. Of course guests could try to land a largemouth bass to beat the lake record of 14.02 pounds, cook it on your grill and eat at the picnic table while enjoying the wildlife.

Rod assists in arranging tours for guests and will arrange a dinner party should you so desire. Nacogdoches was named for the Nacogdoche Indians, and some of the state's most historic landmarks are located here. Guests can visit Stephen F. Austin State University campus and view the memorial erected to L. T. Barret who drilled Texas' first oil well in September 1866 (it came in at 10 barrels a day!)

The apartment consists of two bedrooms, a living room and a kitchenette. Breakfast fixings are in the refrigerator for preparation whenever the mood strikes you. Snacks, beverages and complimentary wine are also provided for guests.

Smoking is limited to the outdoors. Children and pets are welcome. Reservations are required. Guests staying longer receive the seventh night free. The rates are for single/double occupancy and each additional guests is charged $10.

Directions: Ten miles from Loop 224 on Lake Nacogdoches.

HARDEMAN GUEST HOUSE

316 N. Church St
Nacogdoches 75961
Reservations: 409 569 1947

Innkeeper: Lea Smith, Resident Owner
Open: All Year
Facilities: 4 Bedrooms, All Private Baths
Breakfast: Full
Rates: $65 - $80 For 2 Guests
Payment: MC,Visa,Check

Built in 1892 by Robert Lee Hardeman, this renovated, two story home surrounded by pecan, pin oaks, dogwoods and blooming hibiscus is located in the Old Washington Square Historic District. The Caddo Indians established the area as a ceremonial site between 1250 and 1450 A.D. A mound located on the Hardeman property was excavated in the 1930's.

Antiques and reproductions enhanced by the Smith collections, create a homey atmosphere of comfort and relaxation. The English Room furnished with walnut Edwardian pieces is decorated in green, burgundy and rose with Queen bed and private bath. The Oriental Room with a color scheme of black, white and red portrays the simple elegance of the name. A Geisha Girl quilted wall hanging and collection of porcelain are featured. The French Room creates a feeling of romance with its French provincial flair, colors of beige, forest green and peach, and Berkey and Gay furniture. Or enjoy the American art pottery, quilts and antiques in the Americana Room reminiscent of Grandma's House.

A sumptuous breakfast including home baked breads, and home made jams/jellies is served on fine china, crystal and sterling silver from 8-9 a.m. in the dining room. Coffee and tea are available on the stair landing beginning at 6:45 a.m.

Smoking is prohibited. If you are comfortable with your child in these surroundings, then your hostess will be comfortable, too. Although she doesn't encourage pets, Lea will accept well-behaved ones who don't know that they are animals! Reservations are required. Special rates for business and extended stays.

MOUND STREET BED & BREAKFAST
408 N. Mound Street
Nacogdoches 75961
Reservations: 409 569 2211

Innkeeper:	Bob Wood, Manager
Open:	All Year
Facilities:	4 Bedrooms, 1 Suite
	3 Private Baths, 1 Shared
Breakfast:	Continental Plus
Rates:	$65 - $110 For 2 Guests
Payment:	MC,Visa,Check

PINE CREEK LODGE
Route 3, Box 1238
Nacogdoches 75964
Reservations: 409 560 6282

Innkeeper:	Elmer Pitts, Resident Owner
Open:	All Year
Facilities:	3 Bedrooms, All Private Baths
Breakfast:	Full
Rates:	$55 - $65 For 2 Guests
Payment:	MC,Visa,Amex,Check

 **Navasota**

THE CASTLE INN BED & BREAKFAST
1403 E. Washington
Navasota 77868
Reservations: 409 825 8051

Innkeepers:	Maj.Gen.Eugene & Joyce Daniel
Open:	All Year
Facilities:	4 Bedrooms, All Private Baths
Breakfast:	Continental Plus
Rates:	$94 For 2 Guests
Payment:	Check

New Braunfels

ANTIK HAUS BED & BREAKFAST

118 S. Union
New Braunfels 78130
Reservations: 210 625 6666

Innkeepers:	Donna & Jim Irwin, Resident Owners
Open:	All Year
Facilities:	4 Bedrooms, 2 Shared Baths
Breakfast:	Gourmet
Rates:	$45 - $80 For 2 Guests
Payment:	Check

AUNT NORA'S BED & BREAKFAST

120 Naked Indian Trail
New Braunfels 78132
Reservations: 800 687 2887/2l10 905 3989

Innkeepers:	Alton & Iralee Haley, Resident Owners
Open:	All Year
Facilities:	1 Bedroom with Pvt Bath
	Plus Four 1Bed-1bath Cottages
Breakfast:	Full
Rates:	$85 - $150 For 2 Guests
Payment:	Check

FAUST HOTEL

240 S. Seguin
New Braunfels 78130
Reservations: 512 625 7791

Innkeeper:	Cathy Carpenter, Manager
Open:	All Year
Facilities:	21 Bedrooms, All Private Baths
Breakfast:	Continental Plus
Rates:	$49 - $59 For 2 Guests
Payment:	All Major,Check

GRUENE COUNTRY HOMESTEAD INN

832 Gruene Road
New Braunfels 78130
Reservations: 210 606 0216

Innkeepers:	Billie & Ed Miles
	Resident Owners
Open:	All Year
Facilities:	9 Bedrooms, All Private Baths
Breakfast:	Continental Plus
Rates:	$95 - $115 For 2 Guests
Payment:	Check

Gruene Country Homestead, built in the 1860's of adobe brick, cedar beams and barn wood by German settlers, is known locally as the house that has "moved around town". Its location has been moved, let's see, about four times over the years! You could say this house has moved with the times.

Currently, the homestead has three units in the main house and five units in the fachwerk-style farmhouse. Owners Ed and Billie Miles renovated the vintage buildings to reflect the tastes of the era while providing modern-day comforts. Each unit has its own outside entry and private bath (some have a whirlpool!). Each of the bedrooms has its own distinctive character. The names speak for themselves: The Judge's Chambers, Oma's Suite, The Garden Room, The Cottage, Scarlett's Suite, The Back Room, The Angels' Room and Miss Lili's Room.

The living and dining rooms of the main house are common areas for all guests. A generous Continental Plus breakfast is served in the main dining room each morning. Guests have the use of the porches and grounds.

Smoking and pets are prohibited and the Inn is not appropriate for children under twelve. Reservations are required. Check in after 2 p.m. and check out by 11 a.m. There is a two night minimum stay on weekends and holidays.

Directions: Exit 35 on 337 and go West to Hanz Drive and Right on Gruene Road Take an immediate Left into driveway.

Member: Professional Assn of Innkeepers Int'l

HISTORIC KUEBLER-WALDRIP HAUS

1620 Hueco Springs Loop Rd
New Braunfels 78130
Reservations: 210 625 8372/800 299 8372

Innkeepers:	Margaret & Darrell Waldrip
	Resident Owners
Open:	All Year
Facilities:	8 Bedrooms, All Private Baths
Breakfast:	Full
Rates:	$89 - $200 For 2 Guests
Payment:	All Major, Check

KARBACH HAUS BED & BREAKFAST HOME

487 W. San Antonio Street
New Braunfels 78130
Reservations: 210 625 2131/800 972 5941

Innkeepers:	Capt. BJ And Kathleen Kinney
	Resident Owners
Open:	All Year
Facilities:	Four Bedrooms, All Private Baths
Breakfast:	Gourmet
Rates:	$85 - $110 For 2 Guests
Payment:	MC,Visa,Check

OAK HILL ESTATES BED & BREAKFAST

1355 River Road
New Braunfels 78132
Reservations: 210 625 3170

Innkeeper:	Robbie Borchers, Resident Owner
Open:	All Year
Facilities:	2 Bedrooms, 2 Pvt Baths
	Plus 1 Bed-1 Bath Cottage
Breakfast:	Continental Plus
Rates:	$55 - $145 For 2 Guests
Payment:	Check

PRINCE SOLMS INN

295 East San Antonio Street
New Braunfels 78130
Reservations: 210 625 9169/800 625 9169

Innkeeper:	Carmen Morales, Manager
Open:	All Year
Facilities:	10 Bedrooms, All Private Baths
Breakfast:	Continental Plus
Rates:	$60 - $140 For 2 Guests
Payment:	All Major, Check

RIVER HAUS BED & BREAKFAST
817 E. Zipp Road
New Braunfels 78130
Reservations: 210 625 6411

Innkeepers:	Dick & Arlene Buhl, Resident Owners
Open:	All Year
Facilities:	1 Bedroom With Private Bath
Breakfast:	Full
Rates:	$75 For 2 Guests
Payment:	Inquire

RIVERSIDE HAVEN BED & BREAKFAST
1491 Edwards Blvd
New Braunfels 78132
Reservations: 210 625 5823

Innkeepers:	Tom & Maria Halbrook Resident Owners
Open:	All Year
Facilities:	4 Bedrooms, All Private Baths
Breakfast:	Gourmet
Rates:	$70 - $105 For 2 Guests
Payment:	Check

THE ROSE GARDEN

195 S. Academy
New Braunfels 78130
Reservations: 210 629 3296

Innkeeper:	Dawn Mann, Resident Owner
Open:	All Year
Facilities:	2 Bedrooms, All Private Baths
Breakfast:	Gourmet
Rates:	$65 - $105 For 2 Guests
Payment:	Check

THE WHITE HOUSE BED & BREAKFAST

217 Mittman Circle
New Braunfels 78132
Reservations: 210 629 9354

Innkeepers:	Jerry & Beverly White
	Resident Owners
Open:	All Year
Facilities:	3 Bedrooms, 1 Pvt Bath, 2 Shared
Breakfast:	Full
Rates:	$45 - $70 Fo4 2 Guests
Payment:	MC,Visa,Check

Odessa

K-BAR HUNTING LODGE

15448A South Jasper Ave
Odessa 79763
Reservations: 915 580 5880

Innkeeper:	Camilla Blain, Resident Owner
Open:	All Year
Facilities:	4 Bedroom, 3 Bath Lodge
Breakfast:	Full
Rates:	$70 - $166 Per Guest
Payment:	MC,Visa,Amex,Check

K-Bar Hunting Lodge is part of a working West Texas ranch of over 44,000 acres, a couple of thousand cattle and an active oil field. Nestled in and around the sand dunes about 15 miles South of Odessa, the ranch has a wide variety of native wildlife and a 700-acre game preserve stocked with more than a dozen varieties of European, Asian and African animals.

The hunting lodge can accommodate up to 14 people in the four bedroom, three bath facility. Meals are family style in the lodge under the gaze of about 1000 pairs of eyes from the Blain's extensive taxidermy collection of North American animals, many of whom hang out on the indoor mountain, complete with waterfall!

Guests can stay overnight with breakfast included or, if they prefer, can spend a full day with ranch entertainment and three full meals. Snacks and beverages are also provided. The ranch activities included in the full day plan encompass a challenging sporting clay course, searching for Indian artifacts or fossils in a 200-million year old geological formation, observing the cowboys at work, relaxing in the hot tub on the balcony, or perhaps you would like to hunt a Russian boar? A variety of packages are offered.

Smoking outside only. Accommodations are not appropriate for children. Dogs are allowed in Bunkhouse. Reservations are required.

Directions: From I-20 in Odessa, take Hwy 385 South approximately 12 miles. Turn Right on Apple Street by Wilson's Corner Store. Go West on Apple for several miles until road deadends at Jasper. Turn Right to K-Bar Ranch entrance and follow signs to Lodge.

Olton

THE WILD PLUM BED & BREAKFAST
708 Main Street
Olton 76064
Reservations: 806 285 3014

Innkeeper:	Barbara McFadden
Open:	All Year
Facilities:	7 Bedrooms, All Private Baths
Breakfast:	Full
Rates:	$50 - $55 For 2 Guests
Payment:	MC,Visa,Check

Omaha

SHERWOOD FARM RETREAT
3 Mi. North On Highway 144
Omaha 75571
Reservations: 903 884 3039

Innkeepers:	Jerry & Pat Henderson
	Resident Owners
Open:	All Year
Facilities:	Two 1 Bed-1 Bath Cottages
Breakfast:	Continental
Rates:	$55 - $75 For 2 Guests
Payment:	MC,Visa,Disc,Check

Padre Island N.

LA MANSION BED & BREAKFAST
On Canal Padre Island
Padre Island, N. 78597
Reservations: 512 853 1222

Innkeepers:	Jackie & John Fisher, Owners
Open:	All Year
Facilities:	1 Bedroom With Private Bath
Breakfast:	Continental Plus
Rates:	$93 - $96 For 2 Guests
Payment:	Check For Deposit

Padre Island S.

BROWN PELICAN INN
207 W. Aries
Padre Island, S. 78597
Reservations: 210 761 2722/210 423 5239

Innkeeper:	Vicky Conway, Resident Owner
Open:	All Year
Facilities:	8 Bedrooms , All Private Baths
Breakfast:	Continental Plus
Rates:	$70 - $150 For 2 Guests
Payment:	MC,Visa,Check

MOONRAKER BED & BREAKFAST

107 E. Marisol
Padre Island, S. 78597
Reservations: 210 761 2206

Innkeepers:	Robert & Marcia Burns
	Resident Owners
Open:	All Year
Facilities:	3 Bedrooms, All Private Baths
Breakfast:	Gourmet
Rates:	$125 Fo4 2 Guests
Payment:	MC,Visa,Check

 **Paige**

THE CEDAR LODGE

Rt 1, Box 22A
Paige 78659
Reservations: 512 253 6575

Innkeepers:	Dan & Carol Elkins, Resident Owners
Open:	All Year
Facilities:	4 Bedroom, 1.5 Bath Cabin
	Plus 2 Bed -1 Bath Cabin
Breakfast:	Full & OYO
Rates:	$45 - $65 For 2 Guests
Payment:	Check

Paint Rock

CHAPPARAL RANCH BED & BREAKFAST
9 Mi. West Of Town
Paint Rock 76866
Reservations: 915 732 4225

Innkeepers:	Joe & Nancy Brosig, Resident Owners
Open:	All Year
Facilities:	4 Bedrooms, All Private Baths
Breakfast:	Continental Plus
Rates:	$45 For 2 Guests
Payment:	Check

LIPAN RANCH BED & BREAKFAST
Rt. 1, Box 21C
Paint Rock 76866
Reservations: 915 468 2571/915 732 4386

Innkeepers:	E.H.& Cecelia Brosig, Resident Owners
Open:	All Year W/Exceptions
Facilities:	1 Bedroom With Private Bath
Breakfast:	OYO
Rates:	$45 For 2 Guests
Payment:	Check

 **Palestine**

ASH-BOWERS JARRETT MANSION
301 South Magnolia
Palestine 75801
Reservations: 800 729 4607

Innkeeper:	Jim Jarrett, Resident Owner
Open:	All Year
Facilities:	4 Bedrooms, 2 Shared Baths
Breakfast:	Full
Rates:	$60 For 2 Guests
Payment:	Check

BAILEY'S BUNKHOUSE BED & BREAKFAST
Rt. 7, Box 7618
Palestine 75801
Reservations: 903 549 2028/903 549 2059

Innkeepers:	Jan & Bill Bailey, Resident Owners
Open:	All Year
Facilities:	2 Bedrooms Down
	Plus Loft with Shared Bath
Breakfast:	Continental Plus
Rates:	$50 For 2 Guests
Payment:	Check

COUNTRY CHRISTMAS TREE FARM
516 N. Sycamore
Palestine 75801
Reservations: 800 292 8401

Innkeepers:	Lloyd & Wanda Wilkinson, Owners
Open:	All Year
Facilities:	11 Bedrooms, 7 Pvt Baths, 2 Shared
Breakfast:	Continental Plus Or Full
Rates:	$60 For 2 Guests
Payment:	MC,Visa,Check

THE WIFFLETREE INN
1001 North Sycamore
Palestine 75801
Reservations: 903 723 6793

Innkeepers:	Steve & Jan Frisch, Resident Owners
Open:	All Year
Facilities:	4 Bedrooms, 2 Pvt Baths, 1 Shared
Breakfast:	Full
Rates:	$65 For 2 Guests
Payment:	MC,Visa,Check

Paris

BLODGETT BED & BREAKFAST
750 Pine Bluff
Paris 75460
Reservations: 903 737 0937

Innkeepers:	Mark & Carron Blodgett. Res. Owners
Open:	All Year
Facilities:	2 Bedrooms, 1 Shared Bath
Breakfast:	Continental Plus or Full
Rates:	Call Innkeeper
Payment:	Check

THE OLD MAGNOLIA HOUSE
731 Clarksville Street
Paris 75460
Reservations: 903 785 5593

Innkeepers:	Robbie & Teresa Wright
	Resident Owners
Open:	All Year
Facilities:	3 Bedrooms, All Private Baths
Breakfast:	Continental or Full
Rates:	$60 - $80 For 2 Guests
Payment:	MC,Visa,Amex

 **Pasadena**

SHEEPFOLD FARM & COTTAGE INN

412 E. Harris
Pasadena 77506
Reservations: 713 473 4916

Innkeepers:	Janet Harris & Son Chris
	Resident Owners
Open:	All Year
Facilities:	1 Suite With Private Bath
Breakfast:	Continental Plus
Rates:	$65 - $115 For 1-5 Guests
Payment:	All Major, Check

**Special****: Mention this book when making your reservation and receive fresh fruit in your room.**

Situated in the heart of the city's "Historical District", The Sheepfold Farm & Cottage was once a country home. Built in 1936 by oil roughneck, Mac McNeal, for his lovely "Miss San Antonio 1934" bride, this charming cottage sat on several acres of undeveloped prairieland and was home to ducks, chickens, a WW II "Victory Vegetable Garden" and some of the best strawberry patches around.

Today The Sheepfold sits in a corner plot on one quarter of its original acreage and is home to the Harris family, their dog and cat, several rose bushes, a renewed "Victory Garden", a 60 year old pecan tree producing the sweetest pecans in Texas, and a delightful "fold" of sheep. The 1930's decor is enhanced with arts and crafts collected by your hostess, Janet Harris (once an actress in Hollywood) from all over the world.

The suite consists of three rooms with bedroom, sitting room and private Victorian bath. Janet is well able to provide for her guests comfort with flair and style, having also worked for Chasen's Restaurant in Beverly Hills catering parties for the"Rich and Famous". Weddings arrangements at the Sheepfold include Bride's changing room, complimentary English sixpence for her shoe and use of the home's china and silver. Ask Janet about the "extras" that go with the "Bridal Suite". All guests receive fresh flowers in the room, chocolates on the pillow, cookies by the bedside and a basket of toiletries. What hospitality!! Snacks, beverages and afternoon tea are provided. Smoking is restricted to the front porch. Small well-behaved children are welcome. Inquire about pets. Reservations required.

Member: Texas Bed & Breakfast Society

**Pettus**

THE VICTORIAN MANOR
Main Street
Pettus 78146
Reservations: 512 375 2830/375 2200

Innkeeper:	Desiree Vrazel, Manager
Open:	All Year
Facilities:	2 Bedrooms, All Private Bath
Breakfast:	Full
Rates:	$45 - 460 For 2 Guests
Payment:	All Major, Check

**Pipe Creek**

LIGHTNING RANCH
FM 1283
Pipe Creek 78063
Reservations: 210 535 4096

Innkeeper:	Sybil Broyles, Resident Owner
Open:	All Year
Facilities:	Two 2 Bed-2 Bath Guest Houses
	One 1 Bed-1bath Guest House
Breakfast:	OYO
Rates:	$75 - $90 For 2 Guests
Payment:	Check

 **Pittsburg**

CARSON HOUSE BED & BREAKFAST

302 Mt. Pleasant St
Pittsburg 75686
Reservations: 903 856 2468

Innkeepers:	Cindy & Brian Gornick
	Resident Owners
Open:	All Year
Facilities:	4 Bedrooms, 2 Pvt Baths, 1 Shared
Breakfast:	Full
Rates:	$49 - $69 For 2 Guests
Payment:	Most Major, Check

TEXAS STREET BED & BREAKFAST

218 N. Texas St
Pittsburg 75686
Reservations: 903 856 7552

Innkeepers:	Roy & Debie Knox, Resident Owners
Open:	All Year
Facilities:	6 Bedrooms, All Private Baths
Breakfast:	Continental Plus
Rates:	$59 - $89 For 2 Guests
Payment:	MC,Visa,Check

 # Plano

THE CARPENTER HOUSE
1211 East 16th Street
Plano 75074
Reservations: 214 424 1889

Innkeeper:	Yvonne Grueder, Resident Owner
Open:	All Year
Facilities:	4 Bedrooms, All Private Hallway Baths
Breakfast:	Full
Rates:	$95 For 2 Guests
Payment:	MC,Visa,Amex,Check

 # Port Aransas

HARBOR VIEW BED & BREAKFAST
340 Cotter
Port Aransas 78373
Reservations: 512 749 4294

Innkeepers:	Marlene & Jim Urban, Resident Owners
Open:	All Year
Facilities:	4 Bedrooms, 1 Pvt Bath, 1 Shared
Breakfast:	Full
Rates:	$75 - $90 For 2 Guests
Payment:	Check

SEA SONG BED & BREAKFAST

On Gulf Of Mexico
Port Aransas 78373
Reservations: (512) 853 1222

Innkeeper:	Mitzi Staewen, Resident Owner
Open:	All Year
Facilities:	3 Bedrooms, 1 Shared Bath
Breakfast:	Full
Rates:	$87 - $90 For 2 Guests
Payment:	Check For Deposit

 # Port Arthur

CAJUN CABINS

1900 Martin Luther King
Port Arthur 77640
Reservations: 800 554 3169/409 982 6050

Innkeepers:	Patty & Jerry Oltremari
	Resident Owners
Open:	All Year
Facilities:	19 1 Bed-1 Bath Cabins
Breakfast:	Continental Plus
Rates:	$55 - $65 For 2 Guests
Payment:	All Major,Check

# Quihi
(In Medina County - West of San Antonio)

THE OEFINGER HAUS
FM 471, 2 Mi. East Of Town
Quihi
Reservations: 210 538 2441/741 2949

Innkeeper:	Bonnie Jaks, Manager
Open:	All Year
Facilities:	3 Bedroom, 1 Bath House
Breakfast:	OYO
Rates:	$75 For 2 Guests
Payment:	MC, Visa, Check

# Quitaque

DALE & DONNA'S
BED & BREAKFAST RANCH
Highway 86
Quitaque 79255
Reservations: 806 455 1259

Innkeepers:	Dale & Donna Smith, Resident Owners
Open:	All Year
Facilities:	2 Bedrooms, 1 Shared Bath
Breakfast:	Full
Rates:	$45 - $80 For 2 Guests
Payment:	Check

QUITAQUE QUAIL LODGE

3 Mi. West on Hwy 86
Quitaque 79255
Reservations: 806 455 1261

Innkeepers:	Vinita Floye & Gus Hrncir
	Resident Owners
Open:	All Year
Facilities:	7 Bedrooms, 2 Pvt Baths, 2 Shared
Breakfast:	Full
Rates:	$59 - $69 For 2 Guests
Payment:	Check

Raymondville

THE INN AT EL CANELO

10 Mi. North Of Town
Raymondville 78580
Reservations: 210 689 5042

Innkeepers:	Monica & Ray Burdette
	Resident Owners
Open:	All Year
Facilities:	4 Bedrooms, All Private Baths
Breakfast:	Full - Incl. Dinner
Rates:	$150 For 2 Guests
Payment:	Check

 **Rio Frio**

CASA RIO FRIO
County Route 350
Rio Frio 78879
Reservations: 210 966 2320

Innkeepers:	Leann & Anthony Sharp, Managers
Open:	All Year
Facilities:	3 Bedroom House With 1 Bath
Breakfast:	OYO
Rates:	$145 For 4 Guests
Payment:	Check

DETERING RANCH BED & BREAKFAST
4 Mi. West Of Hwy 83
Rio Frio 78879
Reservations: 210 966 2320

Innkeepers:	Leeann & Anthony Sharp, Managers
Open:	All Year
Facilities:	2 Bed-1 Bath Cottage
	3 Bed-2 Bath Lodge
Breakfast:	Continental
Rates:	$130 For 2 Guests
Payment:	Check

Rio Grande City

LA BORDE HOUSE
601 E. Main Street
Rio Grande City 78582
Reservations: 210 487 5101

Innkeeper:	Mandy Garza, Manager
Open:	All Year
Facilities:	16 Bedrooms, All Private Baths
Breakfast:	Continental
Rates:	$40 - $59 For 2 Guests
Payment:	All Major, Check

Rio Medina

THE HABY SETTLEMENT INN
3980 FM 471 N.
Rio Medina 78066
Reservations: 210 538 2441/210 538 3911

Innkeepers:	Paul & Bonnie Jaks, Owners
Open:	All Year
Facilities:	3 Bedroom, 1 Bath Farm House
Breakfast:	OYO
Rates:	$75 For 2 Guests
Payment:	All Major, Check

Rockport

BLUE HERON INN

801 Patton Street
Rockport 78382
Reservations: 512 729 7526

Innkeepers:	Nancy & Gary Cooper
	Resident Owners
Open:	All Year
Facilities:	4 Bedrooms
	3 Pvt Baths, 1 Shared
Breakfast:	Gourmet
Rates:	$80 - $90 For 2 Guests
Payment:	MC,Visa,Check

Just across the street from the Rockport Beach sits the charming Blue Heron Inn Bed & Breakfast. Purchased by the Cooper's in 1993 and personally updated to its current comfortable state, the talents of local artists are featured and displayed throughout the guest rooms and common living area.

The Federal style house was built by Oklahoma developer Bates McFarland in 1890. Although the residence withstood the famous 1919 hurricane, it sustained serious damage, and major restructuring was orchestrated in the early 1930's. Brick veneer was added, and the many porches and verandas were reconstructed so that guests can now sit and enjoy the Little Bay waters and watch the beauty of large blue herons as they soar over the Rockport Beach and bird island.

The Inn features a large common living room with fireplace, game table and comfortable seating, formal dining room, garden room, attractive grounds with palm and live oak trees, bird viewing and patio seating, and rose and herb gardens. Guests choose between The Bay Room with King bed, scenic view of Little Bay and beach and private bath; The Beach Room with Queen bed, views, large deck and full bath; The Harbor Room with Queen bed, scenic views, large deck, and The Treehouse Room with twin beds overlooking the garden with private bath.

A creative gourmet breakfast is served. Special diets are accommodated with advance notice. Refreshments and home made goodies offered upon arrival at 3 p.m. Check out time is 11 a.m.

The Inn cannot accommodate children, pets or smoking guests

Member: Texas Hotel/Motel Association

ANTHONY'S BY THE SEA

732 S. Pearl Street
Rockport 78382
Reservations: 512 729 6100

Innkeepers:	Denis & Anthony, Resident Owners
Open:	All Year
Facilities:	4 Bedrooms, 2 Pvt Baths, 1 Shared
Breakfast:	Gourmet
Rates:	$55 - $75 For 2 Guests
Payment:	Inqurie

Rockdale

RAINBOW COURTS BED & BREAKFAST

915 E. Cameron
Rockdale 76567
Reservations: 512 446 2361

Innkeepers:	Joan & Dan Ratliffe, Resident Owners
Open:	All Year
Facilities:	1 Suite With Private Bath
Breakfast:	Continental Plus
Rates:	$59 - $75 For 2 Guests
Payment:	MC,Visa,Amex

Ropesville

MC NABB'S GREEN ACRES
BED & BREAKFAST
Rt. 1, Box 14
Ropesville 79358
Reservations: 806 562 4411

Innkeepers:	Ronnie & Sandra Mc Nabb
	Resident Owners
Open:	All Year
Facilities:	4 Bedrooms, 2 Pvt Baths, 1 Shared
Breakfast:	Full
Rates:	$50 - $75 For 2 Guests
Payment:	Check

Round Rock

ST. CHARLES SQUARE BED & BREAKFAST
8 Chishom Trail Road
Round Rock 78761
Reservations: 512 244 6850

Innkeeper:	Faye Jones, Resident Owner
Open:	All Year
Facilities:	3 Bedrooms, All Private Baths
Breakfast:	Continental
Rates:	$60 - $110 For 2 Guests
Payment:	MC,Visa,Amex,Check

Round Top

BRIARFIELD BED & BREAKFAST

219 FM 954
Round Top 78954
Reservations: 409 249 3973

Innkeepers:	Roland & Mary Nestor Stanhope
Open:	All Year
Facilities:	5 Bedrooms, All Private Baths
Breakfast:	Continental Plus
Rates:	$75 - $85 For 2 Guests
Payment:	Check

BROOMFIELDS BED & BREAKFAST

419 N. Nassau Rd
Round Top 78954
Reservations: 409 249 3706/800 719 5693

Innkeepers:	Julia & Bill Bishop, Resident Owners
Open:	All Year
Facilities:	4 Bedrooms, All Private Baths
Breakfast:	Full
Rates:	$90 - $105 For 2 Guests
Payment:	Check

EIN KLEINES HAUS BED & BREAKFAST

402 N. Live Oak Street, FM 1457
Round Top 78954
Reservations: 409 249 3060

Innkeeper:	Pamela Rafferty, Owner
Open:	All Year
Facilities:	2 Bedroom, 2 Bath Guest House
Breakfast:	OYO
Rates:	$75 - $85 For 2 Guests
Payment:	Check

GINZEL HAUS BED & BREAKFAST

Hwy 237, 1 Mi. SW Of Round Top
Round Top 78954
Reservations: 409 249 3060

Innkeeper:	Emile Schwarz, Owner
Open:	All Year
Facilities:	2 Bedroom, 1 Bath Guest House
Breakfast:	Continental Plus
Rates:	$75 - $85 For 2 Guests
Payment:	Check

HEART OF MY HEART RANCH

403 Florida Chappel Rd
Round Top 78954
Reservations: 409 249 3171/800 327 1242

Innkeepers:	Bill & Francis Harris, Resident Owners
Open:	All Year
Facilities:	17 Bedrooms, All Private Baths
Breakfast:	Gourmet
Rates:	$68 - $125 For 2 Guests
Payment:	All Major, Check

STARLIGHT FARM RETREAT CENTER

6251 Walhalla Rd
Round Top 78954
Reservations: 409 249 5773

Innkeeper:	Kay Weiman, Resident Owner
Open:	All Year
Facilities:	3 Bedrooms, 2 Pvt Bath, 2 Shared
Breakfast:	Continental Plus
Rates:	$40 - $50 For 2 Guests
Payment:	Check

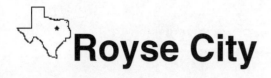

Royse City

COUNTRY LAKE BED & BREAKFAST

FM 2453
Royse City 75189
Reservations: 214 636 2600

Innkeepers: James & Annie Cornelius
Resident Owners
Open: All Year
Facilities: 3 Bedrooms, All Private Baths
Breakfast: Full
Rates: $35 - $85 For 2 Guests
Payment: MC, Visa,Amex,Check

Located on five acres overlooking a private pond, Country Lake Bed & Breakfast, a 1950's style farmhouse, has a library housing a 20 year collection of autographed photos, books and records from the entertainment industry gathered by your host.

Theme oriented rooms include: Happy Trails, a western motif with an autographed poster of Roy Rogers and Trigger, Queen size bed and a "Jacuzzi for two" in its private bath; Mae West features an autographed photo of Mae above the satin headboard on the Queen size bed. Beaded curtains drape the doorway to the fantasy bath where a deep "soaking tub" awaits a bubble bath by candlelight. Europa, soothing in teal green and white, is filled with European artwork and momentos, a carved double bed with featherbed topper, and the bath has a bidet!

Downstairs are two fireplaces, a piano, lots of books, porches, rockers and places to just relax. The "tank" has been stocked and is ready for guests to try a little fishing so bring your poles! Just make yourself at home. That's what James and Annie had in mind when they created the Country Lake Bed and Breakfast.

Guests can request a full breakfast-in-bed (until 10 a.m.) or eat in the fireside room from 8-9:30 a.m. Romantic candlelight dinners (with prior reservation) are served in front of a cozy fireplace. Snacks and beverages are complimentary.

Smoking is not permitted. Children are welcome. Pets are not accommodated. One room is handicap accessible.

Member: Texas Hotel/Motel Assn, East Texas B&B Assn

 # Rusk

BEANS CREEK RANCH BED & BREAKFAST
Rt. 4, Box 411B
Rusk 75785
Reservations: 903 683 6235

Innkeepers:	Louis & Stephane Caveness
	Resident Owners
Open:	All Year
Facilities:	2 Cabins With Pvt Baths
Breakfast:	Continental
Rates:	$50 - $70 For 2 Guests
Payment:	Check

 # Saint Jo

MAIN STREET BED & BREAKFAST
300 South Main Street
Saint Jo 76265
Reservations: 817 995 2127

Innkeeper:	Rhonda Harvill, Owner/Manager
Open:	All Year
Facilities:	6 Bedrooms, 2 Pvt, 2 Shared
Breakfast:	Full
Rates:	$40 - $50 For 2 Guests
Payment:	Check

 **Salado**

COUNTRY PLACE BED & BREAKFAST
Holland Road
Salado 76571
Reservations: 817 947 9683

Innkeepers:	Elinor & Bob Tope, Resident Owners
Open:	All Year
Facilities:	5 Bedrooms, All Private Baths
Breakfast:	Full
Rates:	$75 - $90 For 2 Guests
Payment:	MC,Visa,Check

HALLEY HOUSE BED & BREAKFAST
North Main Street
Salado 76571
Reservations: 817 947 1000

Innkeepers:	Cathy & Larry Sands, Resident Owners
Open:	All Year
Facilities:	7 Bedrooms, All Private Baths
Breakfast:	Gourmet
Rates:	$60 - $105 For 2 Guests
Payment:	All Major, Check

INN ON THE CREEK
Center Circle
Salado 76571
Reservations: 817 947 5554

Innkeepers:	The Epps & The Whislers Resident Owners
Open:	All Year
Facilities:	17 Bedrooms, All Private Baths
Breakfast:	Full
Rates:	$60 - $115 For 2 Guests
Payment:	MC,Visa,Check

 **San Antonio**

ADELYNNE'S SUMMIT HAUS

427 W. Summit
San Antonio 78212
Reservations: 210 736 6272/800 972 7266

Innkeepers:	Adelynne Whitaker
	Resident Owner
Open:	All Year
Facilities:	2 Bedrooms, 2 Private Baths
	Plus 1 Suite , Plus 2 Bedroom -
	1.5 Bath Cottage
Breakfast:	Gourmet
Rates:	$67.50 - $95 For 2 Guests
Payment:	MC,Visa,Amex,Check

A gracious 1920's residence with adjoining "cottage", Adelynne's Summit Haus is furnished with fine Biedermeier antique furniture, crystal, linens, porcelain and a collection of Persian and Oriental rugs.

The main house has a large second floor suite consisting of a master bedroom with King size bed and an adjoining sunroom with double bed. This accommodation is ideal for family and friends traveling together. Two additional bedrooms, also furnished with Biedermeier antiques, complete the extensive upstairs sleeping areas

Adjacent to Summit Haus is a spacious 2,000 square foot "cottage" consisting of a large living area with fireplace, dining room, two bedrooms, bath and a half, breakfast room and full kitchen with laundry facilities. The tree-shaded backyard and deck area add to guests enjoyment of this intimate and private setting. The Cottage is perfect for families or groups who prefer an entire house to themselves at reasonable rates.

Guests at Summit Haus are invited to enjoy the large main parlor with fireplace which is a great setting for special times with friends and family after your day's activities in San Antonio or utilize the outside deck, the perfect place for private conversation under the stars.

Your hostess will provide a European-style breakfast with warm breads and rolls, fresh fruits and juices, a variety of cheeses and cold meats, cereals and yogurt. Complimentary snacks and beverages are provided.

Smoking is restricted to outside decks. Children ten years and older are welcome. There are no provisions for pets. Senior discounts are offered.

Member: PAII, SABBA

BEAUREGARD HOUSE BED & BREAKFAST

215 Beauregard St
San Antonio 78204
Reservations: 210 222 1198

Innkeeper: Sandy Toy, Manager
Open: All Year
Facilities: 3 Bedrooms, All Private Baths
Breakfast: Full
Rates: $85 - $95 For 2 Guests
Payment: MC, Visa, Check

Within the King William Historical District, and only one block away from the famous River Walk, this two story Victorian home was built circa 1910. The home has hardwood floors throughout, and the rooms are filled with furnishings appropriate to the era.

Guests have no need for a car, as this accommodation is one block away from the downtown trolley system that connects this popular historic district to the Alamo, LaVillita, Alamodome, Convention Center Arena, Rivercenter Mall, Market Square and the Spanish Governor's Place, to name just a few attractions.

Anne's Room, which offers a Queen size bed and private bath, is furnished in carefully chosen antique pieces. Beatrice's Room, furnished in white rattan, is like a cool, refreshing breath of spring air and offers a choice of a King bed or two twin beds and a private bath. The General's Room, named in his honor, features a cozy, welcoming fireplace, a Queen size bed and private bath. Laundry facilities are available to guests. Spacious off-street parking with outdoor lighting at night further enhances the convenience and desirability of this location. A full breakfast is served by choice in the dining room, tree-shaded backyard deck or spacious front porch. Snacks and beverages are always available to guests.

Smoking is limited to exterior porches or grounds only. Children are very welcome, but there are no accommodations for pets. Reservations are required. Senior citizen rates are offered, and arrangements may be made for special amenities for special occasions. Check in time is between 4-9 p.m. and check out is at 1 p.m.

BECKMANN INN & CARRIAGE HOUSE

222 E. Guenther St
San Antonio 78204
Reservations: 210 229 1449/800 945 1449

Innkeepers:	Betty Jo & Don Schwartz
	Resident Owners
Open:	All Year
Facilities:	5 Bedrooms, All Private Baths
Breakfast:	Gourmet
Rates:	$80 - $130 For 2 Guests
Payment:	Most Major, Check

Guests to the Beckmann Inn and Carriage House are welcomed with warm and gracious hospitality to a beautiful Victorian home built in 1886. The founder of the Pioneer Flour Mill, C. H. Guenther, gave his daughter, Marie Dorothea, ground from the mill property for a wedding gift. Marie and her husband, Albert Beckmann (an architect) constructed the home. The Pioneer Flour Mill was the nucleus of this affluent German community in the mid 1800's, and very responsible for its development and growth. Albert's parents were the first Germans in San Antonio.

Located in the King William Historic District, across the street from the start of the Riverwalk, and just minutes from the Alamo by trolley, the wonderful wraparound porch welcomes guests to antique-filled rooms featuring ornately carved high back Queen size Victorian beds with private baths.

A gourmet breakfast with a breakfast dessert is served in the formal dining room on china, crystal and silver and includes fresh ground coffee, specialty teas, fruit juice, a main entree, fresh fruit and coffeecake. Guests are also treated to a welcome tea on the front porch.

Smoking is limited to the porches. Children over twelve years can be accommodated. There are no provisions for pets. Mid week specials are based on availability and not offered during special events.

Directions: Exit Durango and go 3 stoplights to S. St. Mary's and turn Left. Immediately take Right on King William and go 5 blocks. Take Left on E. Guenther.

Member: PAII, SABBA, HHAT, THMA

BED & BREAKFAST ON THE RIVER

129 Woodward Place
San Antonio 78210
Reservations: 210 225 6333/800 730 0019

Innkeeper:	Sarah Reddoch, Manager
Open:	All Year
Facilities:	11 Bedrooms, All Private Baths
Breakfast:	Full
Rates:	$79.50 - $150 For 2 Guests
Payment:	All Major, Check

BONNER GARDEN BED & BREAKFAST

145 E. Agarita
San Antonio 78212
Reservations: 210 733 4222/800 396 4222

Innkeepers:	Noel & Jan Stenoien, Resident Owners
Open:	All Year
Facilities:	5 Bedrooms, All Private Baths
Breakfast:	Full
Rates:	$60 - $95 For 2 Guests
Payment:	All Major, Check

BULLIS HOUSE INN

621 Pierce Street
San Antonio 78208
Reservations: 210 223 9426

Innkeepers:	Steve & Alma Cross,Owners
Open:	All Year
Facilities:	7 Bedrooms, 1 Pvt Bath, 3.5 Shared
Breakfast:	Continental Plus
Rates:	$45 - $69 For 2 Guests
Payment:	All Major,Check

BUTTERCUP BED & BREAKFAST

Near Trinity Unviersity
San Antonio
Reservations: 800 814 6116/210 828 3000

Innkeepers:	Camilla Ritchey & Adell
	Resident Owners
Open:	All Year
Facilities:	2 Bedroom, 2 Bath Cottage
Breakfast:	OYO
Rates:	$125 For 2 Guests
Payment:	Check

FALLING PINES BED & BREAKFAST

300 W. French Place
San Antonio 78212
Reservations: 800 880 4580/210 735 1998

Innkeepers:	Bob & Grace Daupert
	Residednt Owners
Open:	All Year
Facilities:	4 Bedrooms, All Private Baths
Breakfast:	Full
Rates:	$100 - $150 For 2 Guests
Payment:	MC,Visa,Amex,Check

JOSKE HOUSE

241 King William
San Antonio 78204
Reservations: 210 271 0706

Innkeeper:	Jessie Simpson, Resident Owner
Open:	All Year
Facilities:	3 Bedrooms, All Private Baths
Breakfast:	Continental Plus
Rates:	$75 - $95 For 2 Guests
Payment:	Check

CLASSIC CHARMS BED & BREAKFAST

302 King William
San Antonio 78204
Reservations: 800 209 7171/210 271 7171

Innkeeper:	Edith Stockhardt
	Resident Owner
Open:	All Year
Facilities:	5 Bedrooms
	4 Pvt Baths, 1 Shared
Breakfast:	Full
Rates:	$59 - $125 For 2 Guests
Payment:	Check

Located on the main street of the King William Historic District (often called the "prettiest street in Texas") you can enjoy the grandeur of a bygone era at Classic Charms Bed and Breakfast, a 1902 two story Victorian home with antique and eclectic furnishings.

Conveniently located only one block from the famous San Antonio Riverwalk, this accommodation is only six blocks from downtown and the convention center and eight blocks from the Alamo and the exciting Mexican Market!

There are five guest bedrooms in the home, some with private baths and some share baths. Some rooms have television, radio and fireplace.

A full breakfast is served to guests in the dining room including gourmet coffee. Snacks and beverages are complimentary.

Provision has been made for smoking on the exterior porches. For the comfort and convenience of all guests, please bring only well behaved children. Pets may be accommodated by prior arrangement. As your hostess, Edith Stockhardt, about special rates for extended stays, senior citizens and off season times.

Public transportation is only two blocks away. Reservations are absolutely necessary. Check in time is between 4 and 10 p.m.

Directions: Downtown. I35 - I37 to Durgano, to South St. Marys, to King William

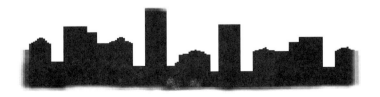

O'CASEY'S BED & BREAKFAST

225 W. Craig Place
San Antonio 78212
Reservations: 800 738 1378

Innkeepers:	John & Linda Casey
	Resident Owners
Open:	All Year
Facilities:	3 Bedrooms, All Private Baths
Breakfast:	Continental Plus
Rates:	$50 - $65 For 2 Guests
Payment:	Check

O'Casey's Bed and Breakfast focuses on coziness and comfort for its guests, say hosts John and Linda Fay Casey.

The 91 year old frame structure offers a spacious front balcony and room porches for visitors to sit back, relax and escape from their busy lives. The home has been updated, but not modernized to the point of losing its character. Guests will find high ceilings, lace curtains, original light fixtures and a stately grand piano.

The accommodation is convenient to three bus lines that make the trip downtown in less than 15 minutes and connect easily to outlying attractions.

The three bedrooms all have private baths. Continental Plus breakfast fare is offered to guests.

No smoking or pets are allowed. Ask the innkeepers about accommodations for children. Reservations are recommended. Tennis and golf facilities are nearby. Weekly Rates receive a 20% discount . Business rates offered (Monday through Thursday) for four night stay.

Directions: One mile North of I-35 between San Pedro and McCullough in the Monte Vista Historical District.

NORTON BRACKENRIDGE HOUSE
230 Madison
San Antonio 78204
Reservations: 210 271 3442/800 221 1412

Innkeepers:	Bennie & Sue Blansett
	Resident Owners
Open:	All Year
Facilities:	5 Bedrooms, All Pvt Baths
	Plus 2 Bed-1bath Guest House
Breakfast:	Full & OYO
Rates:	$89 - $115 For 2 Guests
Payment:	All Major, Check

RIVER HAUS BED & BREAKFAST
107 Woodward Place
San Antonio 78204
Reservations: 210 226 2524

Innkeepers:	William & Cathie Reece
	Resident Owners
Open:	All Year
Facilities:	4 Bedrooms, All Private Baths
Breakfast:	Continental
Rates:	$85 - $104 For 2 Guests
Payment:	All Major

RIVERWALK INN
329 Old Guilbeau St
San Antonio 78204
Reservations: 210 212 8300/800 254 4440

Innkeeper:	Johnny Halpenny, Manager
Open:	All Year
Facilities:	11 Bedrooms, All Private Baths
Breakfast:	Continental Plus
Rates:	$89 - $99 For 2 Guests
Payment:	All Major, Check

SAN ANTONIO YELLOW ROSE

229 Madison
San Antonio 78204
Reservations: 210 229 9903/800 950 9903

Innkeepers:	Jenny & Clif Tice, Resident Owners
Open:	All Year
Facilities:	5 Bedrooms, All Private Baths
Breakfast:	Gourmet
Rates:	$75 - $110 For 2 Guests
Payment:	All Major,Check

THE BELLE OF MONTE VISTA

505 Belknap
San Antonio 78212
Reservations: 210 732 4006

Innkeepers:	Jo Ann & David Bell, III
	Resident Owners
Open:	All Year
Facilities:	8 Bedrooms, 1 Pvt Bath, 3 Shared
Breakfast:	Full
Rates:	$50 - $75 For 2 Guests
Payment:	MC,Visa,Amex,Check

THE PAINTED LADY BED & BREAKFAST

620 Broadway
San Antonio 78215
Reservations: 210 220 1092

Innkeepers:	Cynthia Cesnalis & Linda Shankweiler
	Owner/Managers
Open:	All Year
Facilities:	8 Bedrooms, All Private Baths
Breakfast:	Continental
Rates:	$65 - $200 For 2 Guests
Payment:	All Major,Check

TERRELL CASTLE BED & BREAKFAST

950 E. Grayson St
San Antonio 78208
Reservations: 210 271-9145/210 824 8036

Innkeepers:	Nancy Haley & Katherine Powlis
	Resident Owners
Open:	All Year
Facilities:	4 Bedrooms, 4 Suites
	All Private Baths
Breakfast:	Full
Rates:	$70 - $100 For 2 Guests
Payment:	All Major, Check

"Let our castle be your home", say the hostess' of Terrell Castle on Grayson Street. This 100 year old 26 room Victorian castle with its oriental carpets and period antiques even has a tower and turrets.

There are four rooms and four suites in the "Castle", each with a private bath. On the third floor "The Ballroom Suite" was once the ballroom of the house and boasts an oriental flair with a King size bed in the main room and a twin bed in each of the two alcoves. The Tower Suite encompasses the hexagonal shaped Tower Room which has a King size bed and a twin, and the Moffat Room with its antique French double bed and two twins, a wet bar/vanity area and spacious closets. Worth the climb to the fourth floor, the Americana Room is red, white and blue and has the best views in the house with its antique double platform bed and a twin bed, private bath and a pot bellied stove that works!

Other rooms include the Oval Room with its curved glass windows on each side of the fireplace, a King size bed and the lovely hexagonal Colonial Room with maple furnishings and fireplace.

Breakfast is a feast served in the castle's gigantic dining room, and no one could possibly leave the table hungry.

The "castle" welcomes children and pets (cribs are available). Off season rates are offered. Reservations are necessary. Rates are for double occupancy. Any extra charge of $18 is allocated for each additional person.

THE OGE' HOUSE
ON THE RIVERWALK

209 Washington St
San Antonio 78204
Reservations: 210 223 2353/800 242 2770

Innkeepers:	Patrick & Sharrie Magatagan
	Resident Owners
Open:	All Year
Facilities:	10 Bedrooms, All Private Baths
Breakfast:	Gourmet
Rates:	$110 - $195 For 2 Guests
Payment:	All Major,Check

This elegant and romantic 1857 Ante-bellum mansion is located on one and a half beautifully landscaped acres on the famous San Antonio River-walk, along the tree-lined streets of the King William Historic District (Texas' first and oldest historically designated neighborhood).

The Oge' House is the former home of Texas Ranger and prominent businessman, cattle rancher Louis Oge'. The Inn has a quiet ambiance and is decorated in European and American antiques. The large foyer and library with fireplace and a view of the river are common rooms for guests.

This bed and breakfast locates guests just steps from the Alamo, Convention Center, Alamodome, dining and shopping.

All of the 10 bedrooms have either King or Queen size beds, new private baths, cable color television, telephones and hospitality refrigerators. Seven of the guest rooms have fireplaces, and three have verandas. The suites open onto a porch where guests have a scenic view of old San Antonio.

Your hosts Patrick and Sharrie Magatagan serve breakfast in the beautiful formal dining room or out on the sunny front veranda.

Smoking is allowed outside of the home. The bed and breakfast cannot accommodate young people under 16 years of age. There are no facilities for pets.

Directions: Take Durango exit off I-375 and travel towards town. Turn Left on Pancoast. House is 1st on Right.

Member: HHAT, THMA, PAII, SABBA, IIA and Greater Chamber of San Antonio

THE ROYAL SWAN, A GUEST HOUSE
236 Madison
San Antonio 78204
Reservations: 800 368 3073/210 223 3776

Innkeepers:	Donna West & Carrie Blasic, Owners
Open:	All Year
Facilities:	8 Bedrooms, All Private Baths
Breakfast:	Gourmet
Rates:	$75 - $135 For 2 Guests
Payment:	All Major,Check

THE VICTORIAN LADY INN
421 Howard St
San Antonio 78212
Reservations: 210 224 2524/800 879 7116

Innkeepers:	Joe & Kate Bowski, Resident Owners
Open:	All Year
Facilities:	7 Bedrooms, All Private Baths
Breakfast:	Full
Rates:	$65 - $160 For 2 Guests
Payment:	All Major, Check

 # San Augustine

CAPTAIN E. D. DOWNS HOUSE
301 E. Main
San Augustine 75972
Reservations: 409 275 2289/409 275 5305

Innkeeper:	Dorothy Fussell, Manager
Open:	All Year
Facilities:	3 Bedrooms, 1 Suite
	2 Private Baths, 1 Shared
Breakfast:	Full
Rates:	$55 - $75 For 2 Guests
Payment:	Check

THE WADE HOUSE
202 E. Livingston
San Augustine 75972
Reservations: 409 275 5489/409 275 2553

Innkeepers:	Julia & Nelsyn Wade, Owner
Open:	All Year
Facilities:	5 Bedrooms, 1 Pvt Bath, 2 Shared
Breakfast:	Continental
Rates:	$40 - $80 For 2 Guests
Payment:	MC,Visa,Check

 **San Marcos**

CRYSTAL RIVER INN
326 W. Hopkins
San Marcos 78666
Reservations: 512 396 3739

Innkeepers:	Mike, Cathy & Sarah Dillon
	Resident Owners
Open:	All Year
Facilities:	7 Bedrooms, 4 Suites, All Private Baths
Breakfast:	Full
Rates:	$55 - $110 For 2 Guests
Payment:	All Major,Check

FINER THINGS BED & BREAKFAST
101 Rancho Encino Drive
San Marcos 78666
Reservations: 512 353 2908

Innkeepers:	Pat & Don Klesick, Owner/Managers
Open:	All Year
Facilities:	3 Bedrooms, 1 Pvt Bath, 1 Shared
Breakfast:	Full
Rates:	$85 - $100 For 2 Guests
Payment:	Check

FORGET-ME-NOT RIVER INN

5 Mi. Outside San Marcos On River
San Marcos 78666
Reservations: 512 357 6385

Innkeepers:	Mamie & Edvin Rohlak
	Resident Owners
Open:	All Year
Facilities:	4 Bedrooms, All Private Baths
	Plus 3 Bedroom House
Breakfast:	Full
Rates:	$60 - $90 For 2 Guests
Payment:	Check

LONESOME DOVE BED & BREAKFAST

407 Oakwood Loop
San Marcos 78666
Reservations: 512 392 2921

Innkeepers:	Kim & Carroll Wiley, Resident Owners
Open:	All Year
Facilities:	6 Bedrooms, All Private Baths
Breakfast:	Gourmet
Rates:	$55 - $75 For 2 Guests
Payment:	MC,Visa,Check

TRAILS END BED & BREAKFAST

8909 Ranch Road 12
San Marcos 78666
Reservations: 512 392 0430

Innkeepers:	Tommy & Kathleen Williams
	Resident Owners
Open:	All Year
Facilities:	4 Bedrooms, All Private Baths
Breakfast:	Continental Plus
Rates:	$65 - $85 For 2 Guests
Payment:	MC,Visa,Check

Seabrook

CREW'S QUARTERS
114 Waterfront Drive
Seabrook 77586
Reservations: 713 334 4141

Innkeepers:	Mary & Royston Patterson
	Resident Owners
Open:	All Year
Facilities:	3 Bedrooms, All Private Baths
Breakfast:	Full
Rates:	$40 - $65 For 2 Guests
Payment:	Amex,Check

THE PELICAN HOUSE BED & BREAKFAST
1302 1st Street
Seabrook 77586
Reservations: 713 474 5295

Innkeeper:	Suzanne Silver, Resident Owner
Open:	All Year
Facilities:	4 Bedrooms, All Private Baths
Breakfast:	Gourmet
Rates:	$60 - $70 For 2 Guests
Payment:	All Major, Check

Seadrift

HOTEL LAFITTE

302 Bay Avenue
Seadrift 77983
Reservations: 512 785 2319

Innkeepers:	Frances & Weyman Harding
	Resident Owners
Open:	All Year
Facilities:	10 Bedrooms
	4 Private Baths, 3 Shared
Breakfast:	Full
Rates:	$60 - $115 For 2 Guests
Payment:	MC,Visa,Amex,Check

Hotel Lafitte enjoys a picturesque view of the San Antonio Bay in the quiet fishing village of Seadrift. Built in 1909 and completely restored, this historic hotel is a showplace of period furnishings. The Victorian ambiance is enhanced by a certain mystique. The gracious hotel has been the site of many weddings and special occasions for 80 years. The infamous Bonnie Parker and Clyde Barrow are reported to have spent an anxious night in a room with windows providing a clear view of Bay Street below!

Guests may enjoy a day of fishing, floundering by night, beach combing on Matagorda Island and bird watching at the Aransas Wildlife Refuse. But most of all take time to enjoy this turn-of-the century, charming and unique bed and breakfast.

Your hosts, Frances and Weyman Harding will help you select the accommodation for your perfect retreat. Each floor has different offerings. There are two bedrooms, a picturesque parlor with fireplace, large Victorian lobby, dining room and kitchen on the first floor. The second floor presents eight rooms with varying decor reflecting the gentle mood of the period. The third floor offers two suites with King size beds, one with an oversized Jacuzzi for complete relaxation.

A hearty breakfast is served daily in the dining room, and complimentary wine is served each evening. Snack and beverages are provided to guests.

The Lafitte has no accommodations for children under twelve years or pets. Smoking is permitted. Reservations are required. Special offers are available to groups, business travelers and wedding/birthday packages.

Directions: Highway 185 to Seadrift

 **Seguin**

WEINERT HOUSE BED & BREAKFAST

1207 North Austin Street
Seguin 78155
Reservations: 210 372 0422/800 356 1605

Innkeepers:	Tom & Lynna Thomas
	Resident Owners
Open:	All Year
Facilities:	4 Bedrooms
	2 Private Baths, 1 Shared
Breakfast:	Gourmet
Rates:	$60 - $95 For 2 Guests
Payment:	MC,Visa,Check

Behind the picket fence, among flowers, herbs and a grape arbored walkway, sits the Weinert House Bed & Breakfast. Built in 1895 by Senator F. C. Weinert, a former Secretary of State and distinguished politician locally and statewide, this Queen Anne Victorian home had been continually occupied by family for 97 years. The home is romantic and peaceful, and yet can accommodate the most sophisticated traveler.

Downstairs enjoy the music room with its wind-up Victrola and records, or read and sip something soothing in the parlor while the antique clock chimes the hours away. The formal dining room can be reserved for a special family dinner, and the glass sunroom seats breakfast and tea guests. Play crochet in view of the original smokehouse which still stands on the grounds.

Four beautiful bedrooms, fireplaces and antiques are part of the Weinert House ambiance. The Senator's Suite has a King size brass bed, fireplace, private bath, screened sunporch with wicker furniture and an alcove room with twin beds.

Smoking is not permitted in the house. Children are welcome if ten years or older. Pets need to be left at home. Check in time is between 2-7 p.m. and check out is 11 a.m. Guests staying four nights, receive the fifth night free. Discounts also offered for renting the entire house for a weekend, and corporate rates are extended to business travelers.

Directions: I-10E or W, Exit 609. South on Bus. 123 1 mi. to light - property is 1st Left turn after light.

Member: THMA, HHAT, New Braunfels B&B Assn

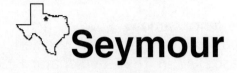# Seymour

OREGON CITY INN HISTORICAL COTTAGE
200 N. East St
Seymour 76380
Reservations: 817 888 3973

Innkeepers:	Ray & Barbara Moore, Owners
Open:	All Year
Facilities:	1 Bedroom, 1 Bath Cottage
Breakfast:	OYO
Rates:	$40 - $60 For 2 Guests
Payment:	Check

# Shafter

CIBOLO CREEK RANCH
Highway 67, 34 Mi. South Of Marfa
Shafter 79850
Reservations: 915 229 3507

Innkeeper:	Jane Shurley, Manager
Open:	All Year
Facilities:	12 Bedrooms, All Private Baths
Breakfast:	Gourmet (All meals Included)
Rates:	$420 - $470
Payment:	MC,Visa,Amex,Check

Sherman

HART'S COUNTRY INN BED & BREAKFAST

601 North Grand Avenue
Sherman 75090
Reservations: 903 892 2271

Innkeepers:	Rhay & Jim Blevins, Resident Owners
Open:	All Year
Facilities:	4 Bedrooms, All Private Baths
Breakfast:	Full
Rates:	$50 For 2 Guests
Payment:	Check

Shiner

OLD KASPER HOUSE BED & BREAKFAST

219 Avenue C
Shiner 77984
Reservations: 512 594 4336

Innkeeper:	Mary Novak, Owner/Manager
Open:	All Year
Facilities:	7 Bedrooms, All Private Baths
Breakfast:	Full
Rates:	$45 - $65 For 2 Guests
Payment:	All Major, Check

 # Silsbee

SHERWOOD TRAIN DEPOT
BED AND BREAKFAST

134 Sherwood Trail
Silsbee 77656
Reservations: 409 385 0188

Innkeeper:	Jerry Allen, Resident Owner
Open:	All Year
Facilities:	1 Bedroom With Private Bath
Breakfast:	Full
Rates:	$60 For 2 Guests
Payment:	Check

Sherwood Train Depot Bed and Breakfast is a two story cypress home in a beautiful wooded setting of beech and oak trees providing a quiet peaceful atmosphere for visitors.

A unique design of knottie cypress wood can be found inside this lovely home. A "G" scale "LGB" train system runs on a cypress ceiling-hung rail system over 350 feet long throughout the home. Its route is through the dining room, kitchen, spiral loops upstairs to the town of Silsbee. Within this town is Santa Fe Freight Station, Kirby Lumber Mill and other buildings. The train system has twelve or more switching spurs all electrically operated from upstairs or downstairs. The train is a logging train with a Western style smoking locomotive with cowcatcher and coal motorized tender all from the 1800's!! Guests will be fascinated with the unusual track layout.

The accommodations at Sherwood Train Depot are homey and comfortable. There's just one bedroom with private bath. Your host can also provide an additional Queen size bed (for two children) in an adjacent room at a nominal fee.

The bed and breakfast provides a full breakfast to guests as well as snacks and beverages. Lunch and dinner may be arranged at an additional cost.

Smoking on porches only. Children are welcome and will be fascinated by this unusual accommodation. Pets can be accommodated on the porches and must be leashed. Reservations are required. A hot tub is on the premises. Clergy receive a special discount, as well as guests who stay three or more nights.

Member: Texas Hotel/Motel Assn

 **Sinton**

GARDEN ACRE BED & BREAKFAST
203 South Bowie
Sinton 78387
Reservations: 512 364 2077

Innkeepers:	Ray McElroy & Betty Wiesner
	Resident Owners
Open:	All Year
Facilities:	2 Bedroom, 1 Bath Pvt Apt
Breakfast:	Continental OYO
Rates:	$70 - $90 For 2 Guests
Payment:	MC,Visa,Check

 **Smithville**

THE KATY HOUSE
201 Ramona Street
Smithville 78957
Reservations: 512 237 4262/800 The Katy

Innkeepers:	Bruce & Sallie Blalock
	Resident Owners
Open:	All Year
Facilities:	4 Bedrooms, All Private Baths
Breakfast:	Full
Rates:	$65 - $85 For 2 Guests
Payment:	Check

# Spring

MC LACHLAN FARM BED & BREAKFAST
24907 Hardy Rd
Spring 77383
Reservations: 713 350 2400

Innkeepers:	Jim & Joycelyn Clairmonte
	Resident Owners
Open:	All Year
Facilities:	4 Bedrooms, 3 Pvt Baths, 2 Shared
Breakfast:	Full
Rates:	$55 - $85 For 2 Guests
Payment:	All Major, Check

# Spur

THE SPUR BUNKHOUSE BED & BREAKFAST
2 Mi. North Of Spur On Hwy 70
Spur 79370
Reservations: 806 271 3429

Innkeepers:	Trey & Mina Pellizzari
	Owner/Managers
Open:	All Year
Facilities:	1 Bedroom, 1 Bath Cottage
Breakfast:	Full
Rates:	$35 - $60 For 2 Guests
Payment:	Check

Stephenville

THE OXFORD HOUSE

563 N. Graham
Stephenville 76401
Reservations: 817 965 6885/817 968 8171

Innkeepers:	Bill & Paula Oxford, Managers
Open:	All Year
Facilities:	4 Bedrooms, All Private Baths
Breakfast:	Full
Rates:	$58 - 75 For 2 Guests
Payment:	MC,Visa,Check

The Oxford House Bed and Breakfast, constructed in 1898 and still in the same family, lies deep in the heart of Texas. The restored two story Victorian home brings to life the ambiance of an affluent family home at the turn of the century. Guests to Judge Oxford's home enjoy the furnishings from the original household, punctuated by antiques purchased to complete the mood. Original portraits decorate the walls, there is a pump organ and a fainting couch, all adding to the romance of this wonderful period in history.

Upstairs there are four cozy bedrooms tastefully decorated with private baths. Fresh flowers, scented soap and bubble bath for your enjoyment will make you feel truly pampered. Outside guests can wile away time on the porch that surrounds most of the house or stroll in the backyard and relax in the gazebo.

Enjoy a home cooked country breakfast served in the home's dining room and prepared by your hostess, Paula Oxford, whose specialties will tempt your tastebuds. Snacks and beverages are complimentary. Guests are offered a glass of wine on their arrival. Honeymoon packages with breakfast in bed and complimentary champagne can be arranged. Your hosts will also prepare special event packages upon request including wedding arrangements.

You may smoke on the porches or in the garden. Children six and over can be accommodated. No pets are allowed. The house is handicap accessible on the lower floor only. Discounts are given to senior citizens. Reservations are required.

Directions: Hwy 377 from Ft. Worth or I-20 to Hwy 281 South

Member: Historic Hotel Association

 # Stonewall

INN ON GRAPE CREEK
Hwy 290, 10 Mi. East Of Fredericksburg
Stonewall 78671
Reservations: 210 644 2710

Innkeeper:	Deborah Schumann, Manager
Open:	All Year
Facilities:	2 Bedrooms, All Private Baths
Breakfast:	Continental Plus
Rates:	$75 For 2 Guests
Payment:	MC,Visa,Check

 # Sulphur Springs

BRIGHT STAR BED & BREAKFAST
438 N. Davis
Sulphur Springs 75482
Reservations: 903 885 8536

Innkeepers:	Eddie & Yvonne Burgess
	Owner/Managers
Open:	All Year
Facilities:	5 Bedrooms, 3 Pvt Baths, 1 Shared
Breakfast:	Full
Rates:	$75 - $95 For 2 Guests
Payment:	MC,Visa,Check

 # Sweetwater

MULBERRY MANOR

1400 Sam Houston
Sweetwater 79556
Reservations: 915 235 3811/800 235 3811

Innkeepers:	Raymond & Beverly Stone
	Resident Owners
Open:	All Year
Facilities:	7 Bedrooms, All Private Baths
Breakfast:	Courmet
Rates:	$55 - $195 For 2 Guests
Payment:	All Major,Check

 # Taylor

CENTURY HOUSE BED & BREAKFAST INN

604 Porter Street
Taylor 76574
Reservations: 512 352 3278

Innkeeper:	Liza Traxler, Owner/Manager
Open:	All Year
Facilities:	4 Bedrooms, 2 Pvt Baths, 1 Shared
Breakfast:	Full
Rates:	$62 - $75 For 2 Guests
Payment:	Check

 # Teague

HUBBARD HOUSE INN BED & BREAKFAST
621 Cedar Street
Teague 75860
Reservations: 817 739 2629/562 2496

Innkeeper:	John Duke, Resident Owner
Open:	All Year
Facilities:	6 Bedrooms, 3 Shared Baths
Breakfast:	Full
Rates:	$60 For 2 Guests
Payment:	MC,Visa, Amex,Check

 # Texarkana

MAIN HOUSE BED & BREAKFAST
3419 Main St
Texarkana 75503
Reservations: 903 793 5027

Innkeepers:	Zona & Jim Farris, Resident Owners
Open:	All Year
Facilities:	2 Bedrooms, 1 Shared Bath
Breakfast:	Gourmet
Rates:	$60 For 2 Guests
Payment:	Check

MANSION ON MAIN BED & BREAKFAST INN

802 Main Street
Texarkana 75501
Reservations: 903 792 1835

Innkeeper:	Joveta Hawthorne, Manager
Open:	All Year
Facilities:	4 Bedrooms, 2 Suites, All Private Baths
Breakfast:	Gourmet
Rates:	$60 - $110 For 2 Guests
Payment:	MC,Visa,Amex,Check

THE FARM HOUSE BED & BREAKFAST

4802 S. Kings Highway
Texarkana 75501
Reservations: 903 838 5454

Innkeepers:	Patricia & Jerry Weldon Resident Owners
Open:	All Year
Facilities:	2 Bedrooms, 1 Shared Bath
Breakfast:	Full
Rates:	$60 For 2 Guests
Payment:	Check

Turkey

HOTEL TURKEY

P.O. Box 37
Turkey 79261
Reservations: 806 423 1151/800 657 7110

Innkeepers:	Scott & Jane Johnson, Resident Owners
Open:	All Year
Facilities:	15 Bedrooms, 12 Pvt Baths, 3 Shared
Breakfast:	Full
Rates:	$59 - $75 For 2 Guests
Payment:	MC,Visa,Amex,Check

CHILTON GRAND BED & BREAKFAST

433 S. Chilton Ave
Tyler 75702
Reservations: 903 595 3270

Innkeepers:	Jerry & Carole Glazebrook
	Resident Owners
Open:	All Year
Facilities:	4 Bedrooms, All Private Baths
Breakfast:	Full
Rates:	$65 - 200 For 2 Guests
Payment:	All Major, Check

Named the Chilton Grand, a Bed and Breakfast Establishment. . . it certainly is GRAND. Situated in the lovely brick streeted Azalea district on what was formerly known as "Silk Stocking Row", this stately two story red brick 1910 Greek Revival Mansion, surrounded by oaks, maple, magnolia and pecan trees, will capture your imagination of days gone by.

Stained and etched glass, stenciling, faux finishes, Trompe l'oeil vines, and wonderful antiques combined with truly elegant decorating by your hostess, Carole Glazebrook, present you with immaculate accommodations of uncompromising quality.

Each guest chamber and private bath has been carefully and lovingly designed to make your stay at Chilton Grand a truly memorable one. Let yourself be pampered with true Southern Hospitality and attentive service by caring hosts.

A 1500 square foot, ten room honeymoon/anniversary/special occasion or no occasion/romantic getaway cottage, "The Ivy Cottage", is also available with a two person Jacuzzi in an indoor "Gazebo Tub Room", an ivy canopied Queen size feather bed and lots of privacy.

Home made stuffed pancakes may be on the menu for breakfast which is served in the dining room.

Reservations are required. For the comfort of guests, no smoking will be allowed in the house. The Grand is not equipped to accommodate small children or pets. Check in is between 3-7 p.m. and check out is at 11 a.m. Business mid week discounts are offered.

Directions: Hwy 31 to Chilton then one block South to 433 S. Chilton

Member: Tyler and East Texas B&B Assns

AZALEA INN BED & BREAKFAST

10886 Spur 164
Tyler 75709
Reservations: 903 595 3610

Innkeepers:	Ruth & Bob Baker, Resident Owners
Open:	All Year
Facilities:	2 Bedrooms, All Private Baths
Breakfast:	Full
Rates:	$95 For 2 Guests
Payment:	MC,Visa,Disc,Check

CHARNWOOD HILL INN

223 E. Charnwood
Tyler 75701
Reservations: 903 597 3980

Innkeeper:	Andy Walker, Resident Owner
Open:	All Year
Facilities:	6 Bedrooms, All Private Baths
Breakfast:	Gourmet
Rates:	$95 - $270 For 2 Guests
Payment:	MC,Visa,Disc,Check

MARY'S ATTIC BED & BREAKFAST

413 S. College
Tyler 75702
Reservations: 903 592 5181

Innkeeper:	Mary Mirsky, Resdient Owenr
Open:	All Year
Facilities:	5 Bedrooms, 2 Pvt Baths, 1 Shared
Breakfast:	OYO
Rates:	$75 For 2 Guests
Payment:	MC,Visa,Disc,Check

THE SEASONS BED & BREAKFAST

313 E. Charnwood
Tyler 75701
Reservations: 903 533 0803

Innkeepers:	Jim & Myra Brown, Resident Owners
Open:	All Year
Facilities:	4 Bedrooms, 2 Pvt Baths, 1 Shared
Breakfast:	Gourmet
Rates:	$95 - $125 For 2 Guests
Payment:	All Major, Check

THE WOLDERT-SPENCE MANOR

611 West Woldert Street
Tyler 75702
Reservations: 903 533 9057

Innkeepers:	Richard & Pat Meaton
	Resident Owners
Open:	All Year
Facilities:	5 Bedrooms, All Private Baths
Breakfast:	Full
Rates:	$75 - $95 For 2 Guests
Payment:	All Major,Check

ROSEVINE INN BED & BREAKFAST

415 South Vine Avenue
Tyler 75702
Reservations: 903 592 2221

Innkeepers:	Bert & Rebecca Powell
	Resident Owners
Open:	All Year
Facilities:	5 Bedrooms, 2 Suites
	All Private Baths
Breakfast:	Gourmet
Rates:	$65 - $150
Payment:	All Major,Check

Rosevine Inn Bed and Breakfast, surrounded by a white picket fence, is a quaint red brick two story home built in the 1920's style located in the Brick Street District, and was Tyler's first bed and breakfast. Hosts Bert and Rebecca Powell will make your stay enjoyable, whether you are on business or just need a getaway.

The Inn offers many amenities including a covered hot tub outdoors, courtyard complete with fountain, a fireplace, a lodge style game room in which you may enjoy billiards, board games, cards, darts, horseshoes and in warmer weather, volleyball and badminton. The fireplaces burn regularly in the courtyard and the gameroom.

The four upstairs rooms are furnished with antiques and have private baths. Two suites with Queen beds are also available, or you may wish to stay in the "barn".

A gourmet breakfast is served in the dining room between 7:30-9:30 a.m. For guests who are early risers, a comfortable nook on the second floor landing has a coffeemaker and a television.

Your hosts will be more than happy to direct you to great restaurants, antique shoppes, museums, lakes, rose gardens and other sites in Tyler and the surrounding area. Business travelers can be accommodated with airport pickup, fax and copy machines, VCR and secretarial services. Groups are welcome. No pets are allowed. Children are welcome with advance arrangement. This is a non-smoking facility. Stay at Rosevine five times and your sixth stay is free.

Member: THMA, PAII, East Texas Assn of B&B, Tyler Hotel/Motel Assn

 **Uncertain**

BLUE HERON INN BED & BREAKFAST
Big Oak Road
Uncertain 75661
Reservations: 903 679 4183

Innkeepers:	Jimmie & Kay Evans, Resident Owners
Open:	All Year
Facilities:	2 Bedroom, 1 Bath Home
Breakfast:	OYO
Rates:	$85 For 2 Guests
Payment:	Check

CADDO COTTAGE BED & BREAKFAST
Mossy Brake Drive
Uncertain 75661
Reservations: 903 789 3988/903 789 3297

Innkeepers:	Pete & Dorothy Grant
	Resident Owners
Open:	All Year
Facilities:	2 Bedroom, 2 Bath Cottage
Breakfast:	OYO
Rates:	$85 For 2 Guests
Payment:	Inquire

CYPRESS MOON COTTAGE
560 Big Oak Rd
Uncertain 75661
Reservations: 903 679 3154

Innkeepers:	True & Lady Margaret Redd, Owners
Open:	All Year
Facilities:	2 Bedroom, 1 Bath Cottage
Breakfast:	Continental
Rates:	$85 For 2 Guests
Payment:	Inquire

MOSSY BRAKE LODGE

Mossy Brake Drive
Uncertain 75661
Reservations: 800 607 6002

Innkeeper:	Norman Presson, Resident Owner
Open:	All Year
Facilities:	1 Bedroom With Private Bath
Breakfast:	Continental Plus
Rates:	$50 For 2 Guests
Payment:	Check

SPATTERDOCK GUEST HOUSE

124 Mossy Brake Dr
Uncertain 75661
Reservations: 903 789 3288

Innkeepers:	Robert & Dottie Russell, Res.Owners
Open:	All Year
Facilities:	3 Bed-1 Bath Lake House
Breakfast:	OYO
Rates:	$85 For 2 Guests
Payment:	Check

Utopia

NEWKIRKS BY THE RIVER

RR 187, 1 Mi West Of Utopia
Utopia 78884
Reservations: 210 966 2320

Innkeepers:	Bill & Helen Newkirk, Resident Owners
Open:	All Year
Facilities:	1 Bedroom With Pvt Bath
Breakfast:	Full
Rates:	$65 For 2 Guests
Payment:	Check

BLUE BIRD HILL BED & BREAKFAST

Hide-Away Cabin

Farm Market Rd 1050
Utopia 78884
Reservations: 512 966 3525/2320

Innkeepers:	B. & Roger Garrison
	Resident Owners
Open:	All Year
Facilities:	2 Bedroom - 1 Bath Suite
	1 Bedroom - 1 Bath Cabin
Breakfast:	Gourmet
Rates:	$65 - $75 For 2 Guests
Payment:	Check

A weathered rustic cedar picket fence surrounds Blue Bird Hill Bed and Breakfast, an early-Texas style German farmhouse (Circa 1972). The Texas Star Suite (sleeps five) has its own outside entry and private deck for star gazing and is decorated with early Texas momentos of pioneer and native Americans. Guests can view distant hills through the tree tops and watch the deer feed.

Guests can utilize the extensive library, visit the Garden Room to relax in the hot tub, sit in front of the fireplace which is ablaze from October to May, or lie in the tree shaded hammock.

A gourmet breakfast is served in the downstairs dining room including goodies such as casseroles or Eggs Benedict, and home baked sweet rolls.

Or how about a very secluded, Hideaway Cabin in the woods with a tin roof and sleeping loft with King size bed, open beamed ceiling and fully furnished kitchen, rag rugs, patchwork quilts and even a RED claw foot tub! On those nippy Hill Country nights, a fireplace cuts the chill and adds a special glow to the atmosphere. In summer cool breezes across the creek are your air conditioning, but the cabin is under huge live oaks and is never hot or humid. You can relax in a private hot tub under the stars or take a dip in the spring fed creek. There's no telephone, no television, just peace, tranquillity and privacy. A full breakfast is provided.

Smoking is prohibited, and pets are not allowed. Children are welcome. Reservations are required. Snacks, beverages, and wine are offered.

Directions: Hwy FM 1050 ten miles West of Utopia.

Member: Frio Canyon Chamber of Commerce

SUNSET RIDGE BED & BREAKFAST

P.O. Box 156
Utopia 78884
Reservations: 210 966 3593

Innkeepers:	Dixie Robins /Temple Johnson,Owners
Open:	All Year
Facilities:	3 Bedrooms, 1 Pvt Bath, 1 Shared
Breakfast:	Continental Plus
Rates:	$75 For 2 Guests
Payment:	Check

UTOPIA ON THE RIVER

2 Mi. South On Hwy 187
Utopia 78884
Reservations: 210 966 2444

Innkeepers:	Aubrey & Polly Smith, Managers
Open:	All Year
Facilities:	12 Bedrooms, All Private Baths
Breakfast:	Full
Rates:	$74 For 2 Guests
Payment:	All Major,Check

 **Uvalde**

CASA DE LEONA BED & BREAKFAST

1149 Pearsall, Hwy 140
Uvalde 78802
Reservations: 512 278 8550

Innkeepers:	Carolyn & Ben Dur, Resident Owners
Open:	All Year
Facilities:	6 Bedrooms, 4 Pvt Baths, 1 Shared
Breakfast:	Gourmet
Rates:	$55 - $150 For 2 Guests
Payment:	MC,Visa,Amex,Check

 # Van Alstyne

DURNING HOUSE BED & BREAKFAST

205 W. Stephens
Van Alstyne 75495
Reservations: 903 482 5188

Innkeepers:	Brenda Hix & Sherry Heath, Owners
Open:	All Year
Facilities:	2 Bedroom, 1 Bath House
Breakfast:	Continental Plus
Rates:	$75 For 2 Guests
Payment:	MC,Visa,Check

 # Vanderpool

TUBBS HERITAGE HOUSE

Old Utopia Road
Vanderpool 78885
Reservations: 210 966 3510

Innkeeper:	Janie Tubbs, Resident Owner
Open:	All Year
Facilities:	3 Bedrooms, 1 Pvt Bath, 1 Shared
Breakfast:	Full
Rates:	$50 - $75 For 2 Guests
Payment:	MC,Visa

TEXAS STAGECOACH INN

Highway 187
Vanderpool 78885
Reservations: 210 966 6272

Innkeepers: David & Karen Camp
                    Resident Owners
Open: All Year
Facilities: 5 Bedrooms
                    1 Private Bath, 2 Shared
Breakfast: Gourmet
Rates: $70 - $90 For 2 Guests
Payment: Check

You can almost hear the "Whoa" as you pass the large iron ring imbedded in the trunk of a massive Oak (used by riders to tie up their horse and wagon in bygone days) at The Texas Stagecoach Inn. The stately white mansion with blue shutters and lots of porch looks down on the Sabinal River outside of Vanderpool. The home is known throughout Texas for the original Thompson family and their hospitality, a tradition being carried on by your hosts, David and Karen Camp.

The "user friendly" 6000 sq.ft. ranch style home, originally built by Robert Hamilton Thompson in 1885, and recently completely renovated by the Camps, has five rooms available for guests. Berber carpet, 1950's era Western furniture from the W. R. Dallas company, Saltillo tile and wonderful French doors lend to this Inn's charm. The house is divided by a gift and gallery area which separates the guest rooms from the family living quarters. An impressive entryway features a massive double fireplace constructed of rock pulled from the river below the house.

A "sunporch with a view" at the rear of the house is used for serving guests a gourmet breakfast and also serves as a common general lounge area for guests to meet and greet. Perhaps Karen will make you one of Aunt Dottie's original recipes which have remained in the house and are cherished as a piece of this incredible heritage. For guests who love history, Karen is indeed a veritable fountain of information.

This is a non-smoking home. The inn can accommodate children ten or older but has no facilities for pets. Reservations are required. The Camps offer discounts to honeymoon couples.

Member: PAII and Chamber of Commerce

**Victoria**

FORREST PLACE SUITES BED & BREAKFAST
507 West Forrest
Victoria 77901
Reservations: 512 578 4260/512 578 0291

Innkeepers:	Leisha & Guy Dioguardi
	Resident Owners
Open:	All Year
Facilities:	3 Suites With Private Baths
Breakfast:	OYO
Rates:	$65 - $105 For 2 Guests
Payment:	MC,Visa,Amex,Check

FRIENDLY OAKS BED & BREAKFAST
210 E. Juan Linn Street
Victoria 77901
Reservations: 512 575 0000

Innkeepers:	Bill & Cee Bee McLeod
	Resident Owners
Open:	All Year
Facilities:	4 Bedrooms, All Private Baths
Breakfast:	Gourmet
Rates:	$55 - $75 For 2 Guests
Payment:	MC,Visa,Check

 **Waco**

THORNTON'S BED & BREAKFAST
908 Speight
Waco 76706
Reservations: 817 756 0273

Innkeepers:	Davis & Jenifer Thornton
	Resident Owners
Open:	All Year
Facilities:	5 Bedrooms, All Private Baths
Breakfast:	Full
Rates:	$69 - $89 For 2 Guests
Payment:	Check

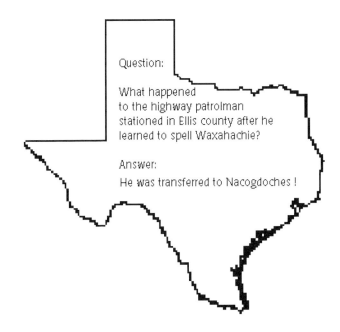

Question:

What happened
to the highway patrolman
stationed in Ellis county after he
learned to spell Waxahachie?

Answer:

He was transferred to Nacogdoches !

COLONIAL HOUSE

2301 Colonial
Waco 76707
Reservations: 817 756 1968

Innkeeper:	Noreen Haney-Kord
	Resident Owner
Open:	All Year except
	Christmas & Thanksgiving
Facilities:	2 Bedrooms Main House
	1 Bedroom, 1 Bath Cottage
Breakfast:	Continental Plus And Full
Rates:	$79 - $89 For 2 Guests
Payment:	Visa,Disc,Check

The first renovations to the Colonial House were found in the 1910 tax records. The original sweeping porches on the front and back were enclosed in 1930. This is a country Georgian style two story elegant home. The home features wood floors throughout, two fireplaces and a parlor which provides a quiet place for guest to relax.

The area attractions are varied and many. You may wish to raft on the Brazos River or do some water skiing, boating or swimming on Lake Waco. History buffs will be interested to learn that a fountain drink mixed in The Old Corner Drug Store in the 1880's was dubbed Dr. Pepper! To this day, the beverage has remained basically unchanged. The museum is housed in the original 1906 bottling plant, now listed on the National Register of Historic Places and well worth a visitor's time. And don't forget the Texas Rangers Museum and the Texas Sports Hall of Fame.

There are two guest bedrooms in the main house and one guest bedroom with private bath in the "cottage".

Guests have a choice of a Continental Plus or a Full breakfast while staying at this bed and breakfast. Your hostess, Noreen Haney-Kord, also provides her guests with afternoon tea and complimentary wine.

Reservations are required. Pets cannot be accommodated. Inquire about suitability for children.

Directions: I-35 South to Waco. Exit at 17th Street and go West (Right) to Waco Street. turn South (Left) to 23rd Street and West (Right) on 23rd to Colonial House

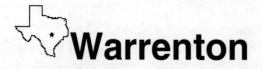# Warrenton

WARRENTON INN BED & BREAKFAST
4339 S. Hwy 237
Warrenton 78961
Reservations: 409 249 3074

Innkeepers:	Carolyn & Ray Fox, Resident Owners
Open:	All Year
Facilities:	5 Bedrooms, 2 Shared Baths
Breakfast:	Full
Rates:	$55 For 2 Guests
Payment:	Check

# Waxahachie

BONNY NOOK INN
414 West Main Street
Waxahachie 75165
Reservations: 214 938 7207/800 486 5936

Innkeepers:	Vaughn & Bonnie Franks
	Resident Owners
Open:	All Year
Facilities:	5 Bedrooms, All Private Baths
Breakfast:	Full
Rates:	$70 - $95 For 2 Guests
Payment:	All Major,Check

MILLIE'S VICTORIAN BED & BREAKFAST

1120 West Jefferson Street
Waxahachie 75165
Reservations: 214 938 7211/800 270 4890

Innkeepers:	Greg & Ginny Timberman
	Resident Owners
Open:	All Year
Facilities:	2 Bedrooms, All Pvt Baths
	Plus 1 Bed-1bath Cottage
Breakfast:	Full
Rates:	$75 - $125 For 2 Guests
Payment:	Check

SEVEN GABLES BED & BREAKFAST

501 North College Street
Waxahachie 75165
Reservations: 214 938 7500

Innkeepers:	Helen & Jim Anderson
	Resident Owners
Open:	All Year
Facilities:	3 Bedrooms, All Private Baths
Breakfast:	Gourmet
Rates:	$75 - $110 For 2 Guests
Payment:	Check

THE CHASKA HOUSE BED & BREAKFAST

716 West Main St
Waxahachie 75165
Reservations: 214 937 3390

Innkeepers:	Louis & Linda Brown, Resident Owners
Open:	All Year
Facilities:	2 Bedrooms, All Private Baths
Breakfast:	Gourmet
Rates:	$80 - $100 For 2 Guests
Payment:	MC,Visa,Amex,Check

THE ROSE OF SHARON BED & BREAKFAST
205 Bryson
Waxahachie 75165
Reservations: 214 938 8833

Innkeepers:	Larry & Sharon Shawn, Res.Owners
Open:	All Year
Facilities:	3 Bedrooms, All Private Baths
Breakfast:	Gourmet
Rates:	$55 - $85 For 2 Guests
Payment:	Check

Weatherford

DERRICK-HOFFMAN fARM
7030 Thorp Spring Rd
Weatherford 76087
Reservations: 817 573 9952/800 573 9953

Innkeepers:	Jean Hoffman & R.V. Derrick Resident Owners
Open:	All Year
Facilities:	4 Bedrooms, 1 Shared Bath
Breakfast:	Full & OYO
Rates:	$70 For 2 Guests
Payment:	Check

ST. BOTOLPH INN BED & BREAKFAST
808 S. Lamar Stret
Weatherford 76086
Reservations: 817 594 1455/800 868 6520

Innkeepers:	Dan & Shay Buttolph, Resident Owners
Open:	All Year
Facilities:	4 Bedrooms, 2 Pvt Baths, 1 Shared
Breakfast:	Full
Rates:	$50 - $85 For 2 Guests
Payment:	MC,Visa,Check

TWO PEARLS BED & BREAKFAST

804 S. Alamo Street
Weatherford 76086
Reservations: 817 596 9316

Innkeepers:	Beth Llewellyn & Janet Davee
	Resident Owners
Open:	All Year
Facilities:	3 Bedrooms, 1 Pvt Bath, 1 Shared
Breakfast:	Full
Rates:	$60 - $75 For 2 Guests
Payment:	MC,Visa,Check

VICTORIAN HOUSE BED & BREAKFAST

1105 Palo Pinto
Weatherford 76086
Reservations: 800 687 1660/817 599 9600

Innkeepers:	Candice & Gregg Barnes, Res.Owners
Open:	All Year
Facilities:	8 Bedrooms, All Private Baths
Breakfast:	Gourmet
Rates:	$89 - $125 For 2 Guests
Payment:	Check

 **West**

ZACHARY DAVIS HOUSE B&B

400 N. Roberts
West 76691
Reservations: 817 826 3953

Innkeeper:	Marjorie Devlin, Resident Owner
Open:	All Year
Facilities:	8 Bedrooms, All Private Baths
Breakfast:	Full
Rates:	$45 - $65 For 2 Guests
Payment:	MC,Visa,Check

Whitesboro

ALEXANDER BED & BREAKFAST ACRES
County Rd 201 At County Rd 212
Whitesboro 76240
Reservations: 903 564 7440/800 887 8794

Innkeepers:	Jim & Pamela Alexander
	Resident Owners
Open:	All Year
Facilities:	5 Bedrooms, All Private Baths
	3 Bed-1 Bath Cottage
Breakfast:	Full
Rates:	$49 - $89 For 2 Guests
Payment:	MC,Visa,Check

LET'ER BUCK BUNKHOUSE
Hw 82 East
Whitesboro 76273
Reservations: 903 564 5701

Innkeeper:	Jean Humphrey, Resident Owner
Open:	Seasonal - March through November
Facilities:	2 Bedrooms, All Private Baths
Breakfast:	Continental Plus
Rates:	$40 For 2 Guests
Payment:	Check

Wichita Falls

HARRISON HOUSE BED & BREAKFAST

2014 11th Street
Wichita Falls 76301
Reservations: 817 322 2299

Innkeepers:	Suzanne Staha & Judith Mc Ginnis
	Resident Owners
Open:	All Year
Facilities:	4 Bedrooms, 2 Shared Baths
Breakfast:	Full
Rates:	$55 - $75 For 2 Guests
Payment:	MC,Visa,Amex,Check

Wimberley

BANDITS HIDEAWAY BED & BREAKFAST

2324 Flite Acres Rd
Wimberley 78676
Reservations: 512 847 9088

Innkeeper:	J. Grimes, Resident Owner
Open:	All Year
Facilities:	2 Bedrooms, All Private Baths
Breakfast:	Continental Plus
Rates:	$70 - $75 For 2 Guests
Payment:	Inquire,Check

BARRISTER'S GUEST QUARTERS
14330 Ranch Road 12
Wimberley 78676
Reservations: 512 847 6211

Innkeeper:	John Buvens, Owner/Manager
Open:	All Year
Facilities:	2 Bedrooms, All Private Baths
Breakfast:	Restaurant Voucher
Rates:	$75 For 2 Guests
Payment:	MC,Visa,Check

BLAIR HOUSE
100 Spoke Hill Rd
Wimberley 78676
Reservations: 512 847 8828

Innkeeper:	Jonnie Standbury, Resident Owner
Open:	All Year
Facilities:	6 Bedrooms, All Private Baths
Breakfast:	Gourmet
Rates:	$135 For 2 Guests
Payment:	MC,Visa,Disc,Check

COTTAGE IN THE DELL
100 Heritage Road
Wimberley 78676
Reservations: 512 847 3330

Innkeeper:	Adelle Turpen, Resident Owner
Open:	All Year
Facilities:	Two 1 Bed - 1 Bath Cottages
Breakfast:	Continental Plus
Rates:	$75 - $85 For 2 Guests
Payment:	Check

DANCING WATER INN

1405 Mt. Sharp Road
Wimberley 78676
Reservations: 512 847 9391

Innkeepers:	Kimberly & David Bear
	Resident Owners
Open:	All Year
Facilities:	4 Bedrooms, All Private Baths
Breakfast:	Continental Plus
Rates:	$65 - $75 For 2 Guests
Payment:	Check

DOBIE HOUSE BED & BREAKFAST

282 Old Kyle Road
Wimberley 78676
Reservations: 512 847 2764

Innkeeper:	Claire Smullen, Owner
Open:	All Year
Facilities:	1 Bedroom, 1 Bath Cottage
Breakfast:	Continental Plus
Rates:	$90 For 2 Guests
Payment:	Visa, Amex,Check

EAGLES NEST BED & BREAKFAST

RR #12
Wimberley 78676
Reservations: 800 460 3909

Innkeepers:	Frank & Jimi Irby, Resident Owners
Open:	All Year
Facilities:	3 Bedrooms, All Private Baths
Breakfast:	Full
Rates:	$60 For 2 Guests
Payment:	MC,Visa,Amex,Check

GUEST HOUSE AT GULLY CREEK
300 Rogers Road
Wimberley 78676
Reservations: 512 847 2953

Innkeeper:	Joy Rogers, Resident Owner
Open:	All Year
Facilities:	1 Bedroom With Pvt Bath
Breakfast:	Continental Plus
Rates:	$80 For 2 Guests
Payment:	All Major, Check

ILA CLAYTON BED & BREAKFAST
300 Green Acres Rd
Wimberley 78676
Reservations: 512 847 9710

Innkeeper:	Ila Clayton, Resident Owner
Open:	All Year
Facilities:	1 Bedroom With Pvt Bath
Breakfast:	Continental Plus
Rates:	$55 For 2 Guests
Payment:	Check

IVY CLIFF COTTAGE
County Rd 281
Wimberley 78676
Reservations: 800 460 3909

Innkeepers:	Pat & Candy Rehmet, Resident Owners
Open:	All Year
Facilities:	Two 1 Bed - 1 Bath Cottages
Breakfast:	Full At Restaurant
Rates:	$100 - $125 For 2 Guests
Payment:	Inquire

OLD OAKS RANCH

5 Mi. North Of Town On CR 221
Wimberley 78676
Reservations: 512 847 9374

Innkeepers:	Bill & Susan Holt
	Resident Owners
Open:	All Year
Facilities:	Three 1 Bedroom, 1 Bath Cottages
Breakfast:	Full At Restaurant
Rates:	$65 - $85 For 2 Guests
Payment:	MC,Visa,Check

RANCHO EL VALLE CHIQUITO
BED AND BREAKFAST RESORT

7 Mi. West Of Town On 2325
Wimberley 78676
Reservations: 512 847 3665

Innkeepers:	Kim & Karon Zombola
	Resident Owners
Open:	All Year
Facilities:	4 Bedrooms, All Private Baths
Breakfast:	Full
Rates:	$75 - $85 For 2 Guests
Payment:	MC,Visa,Amex,Check

RANCHO CAMA BED & BREAKFAST

2595 Flite Acres Rd
Wimberley 78676
Reservations: 512 847 2596/800 594 4501

Innkeepers:	Nell & Curtis Cadenhead
	Resident Owners
Open:	All Year
Facilities:	3 Bedrooms
	1 Private Bath, 1 Shared
Breakfast:	Full
Rates:	$60 - $85 For 2 Guests
Payment:	Check

Peaceful, pastoral, enticing, setting under a canopy of live oaks with abundant swings and rockers from which guests enjoy the panoramic beauty of the Hill Country and adorable miniature horses, donkeys and dwarf goats frolicking at Piddy Paddocks. You're at Rancho Cama Bed & Breakfast.

The Guest House is a cozy, charmingly appointed honeymoon-type cottage accommodating two guests with Queen size bed, sitting area, window seat with library and electric organ.

The Bunkhouse has two rooms with a shared bath. One has extra long twin beds, the other a double bed and bunks. Both rooms may be occupied by guests traveling together and willing to share the bath; otherwise, only one of the two rooms will be rented to allow guests to enjoy a private bath.

Both houses have refrigerator, coffee maker and color cable TV. A beautiful pool and relaxing hot tub are available, although no lifeguard is on duty. Tubing on the beautiful Blanco River and bicycling on country lanes also appeals to guests.

A generous and delicious full breakfast is served beside the pool, weather permitting. On Sunday, breakfast will be served in your room.

Reservations are required. The facility does not accommodate children, pets or smoking. Check in is 4 p.m. and check out is 11 a.m. unless special arrangements have been made.

Directions: From Wimberley Square, South on 12, Left onto 3237, Right onto Hays 173, 2.2 miles on Left.

Member: Wimberley Overnight Association

RIVER BLUFF GUEST COTTAGE

#1 River Bluff Lane
Wimberley 78676
Reservations: 512 847 1524/512 847 3909

Innkeepers:	Chuck & Terri Bursiel
	Resident Owners
Open:	All Year
Facilities:	1 Bedroom, 1 Bath Cottage
Breakfast:	Continental
Rates:	$85 For 2 Guests
Payment:	MC,Visa,Amex

River Bluff Bed and Breakfast is located on a three acre tract of land fronting the beautiful Blanco River. The river front is lined with large cypress trees which create a picturesque environment. There is a quiet picnic and lounging area beneath the trees.

River Bluff offers fishing, swimming, tubing, sightseeing, volleyball and just plain relaxing in peace and quiet. The town of Wimberley is only three miles away and offers a variety of dining, shopping and amateur theater activities. In addition to annual scheduled events, guests can take in the wood caving show at Carousels or the glass blowing show at the Wimberley Glass works. Golfers will find a playing course nearby.

The cottage is contemporary in its design with a rustic environment and can accommodate four adults. The private bedroom, complete bathroom, living area with fireplace and television, fully equipped kitchen including a microwave and a large back screened porch make guests feel welcome and comfortable.

A Continental breakfast of rolls, juice and beverages is provided by hosts Terrie and Chuck Bursiel as well as complimentary wine.

Children are always welcome. Pets and smoking are not allowed. Reservations are required. There is a two night minimum stay. Check in is 3 p.m. and checkout is 12 noon. There is a $10 charge per night for extra persons and a $5 per person day guest charge.

Directions: 2.6 miles out County road 178 from traffic light in Wimberley.

THE HOMESTEAD

RR 12 At CR 316
Wimberley 78676
Reservations: 512 847 8788

Innkeepers:	Clark & Sandi Aylsworth
	Resident Owners
Open:	All Year
Facilities:	Eight 1 Bedroom,
	1 Bath Cottages
Breakfast:	Continental Plus OYO
Rates:	$75 - $95 For 4 Guests
Payment:	Check

The Homestead, consisting of eight fully equipped cottages, is nestled among 100 year old cypress and native pecan trees, along 1000 feet of Cypress Creek. The Creek, which is only 6 miles long and fed from Jacobs Well, is an outlet from the underground aquifer. The crystal clear water flows over small falls and around ancient cypress trees and is swimmable all year round. An abundance of wildlife (birds, fish, deer, etc.) are residents in the area.

Activities include snorkeling, sunbathing, picnicking, nature walking, rafting or just lazing around in one of the beautiful small creek falls. Golf is available at nearby Woodcreek Country Club with a Homestead discount. There is also a hot springs portable spa on the property.

Hosts Sandy and Clark Aylsworth, who have traveled the world and stayed at the "best hotels", have attempted to duplicate the fine service and attention they have received over the years. The property was originally their own "getaway". They now share it with their guests.

Each cabin is 650 - 1000 sq.ft. and has full kitchens with microwaves, cable TV, decks overlooking the creek, Weber grills, fireplaces, telephones and full baths. Breakfast is provided in the refrigerator to be eaten at the convenience of their guests.

Smoking is permitted. Children are warmly welcomed. Pets are allowed in some of the cottages, and one of the cottages is handicap accessible. Reservations are required, and discounts are offered to guests who stay five or more days.

Member: Texas Hotel/Motel Association

THE INN ABOVE ONION CREEK

4444 Highway 150
Wimberley 78676
Reservations: 512 268 1617

Innkeeper:	Suzanne Johnson, Manager
Open:	All Year
Facilities:	6 Bedrooms, All Private Baths
Breakfast:	Full
Rates:	$125 - $225 For 2 Guests
Payment:	MC, Visa,Check

Built in early Texas settler style on 500 acres of Texas Hill Country, The Inn Above Onion Creek is a warm and peaceful spot where travelers can rest in comfort and luxury. Wander through walking trails, venture upon a picnic spot, absorb the colorful wildflowers, shady oaks and cedar elms while keeping an eye out for deer and wild turkey.

Each of the six rooms at the Inn have been meticulously and individually furnished and decorated to tell its own story about its namesake. Your may choose the Tom Martin Room with Queen size bronze bed, antique claw foot tub in a pale moss library-like setting. The Capt. Fergus Kyle Room is downstairs and barrier free with a King size bed, tub-for-two, private porch, large sitting area and bold colors. The Katherine Anne Porter Room has a Queen size sleigh bed, whirlpool tub, two-sided fireplace and crisp yellow and white colors. The M. G. Michaelis Room has a King size long leaf pine Texas Star bed, whirlpool, and private balcony. The Jack Hays Room with King size bed, whirlpool, private balcony and rust and gray colors.The Kuykendall Suite (two stories) has a downstairs sitting room, powder room, upstairs King size iron bed, oversized whirlpool bathroom, double shower, opulent linens and soft moss and honey colors.

Full breakfast including fruit, freshly baked breads and country pastries is served hearthside in the dining room. In the evening, guests are offered a light supper fare of fresh breads, homemade soups and salads.

Reservations are required. No accommodations for children, pets or smoking. Ask about off season rates for multiple nights.

SINGING CYPRESS GARDENS
BED & BREAKFAST
#1 Singing Cypress Gardens
Wimberley 78676
Reservations: 512 847 9344

Innkeepers:	Barbara Ireland-Derr & Robert Ireland
	Resident Owners
Open:	All Year
Facilities:	4 Bedrooms, All Private Baths
Breakfast:	Continental
Rates:	$70 - $125 For 2 Guests
Payment:	MC,Visa,Check

SOUTHWIND BED & BREAKFAST
27012 FM 3237
Wimberley 78676
Reservations: 512 847 5277

Innkeeper:	Carrie Watson, Resident Owner
Open:	All Year
Facilities:	3 Bedrooms, All Private Baths
Breakfast:	Full
Rates:	$70 - $80 For 2 Guests
Payment:	MC,Visa,Disc,Check

STANFIELD'S VUE BED & BREAKFAST
358 Scenic Way
Wimberley 78676
Reservations: 512 842 2787

Innkeeper:	Jackie Stanfield,Resident Owner
Open:	All Year
Facilities:	1 Bedroom, 1 Bath Cottage
Breakfast:	Continental
Rates:	$65 For 2 Guests
Payment:	Check

SUMMER HILL COTTAGE

P.O. Box 1506
Wimberley 78676
Reservations: 512 847 5642

Innkeepers:	John & Michele Gooch
	Resident Owners
Open:	All Year
Facilities:	2 Bedoom, 1 Bath Cottage
Breakfast:	OYO
Rates:	$75 For 2 Guests
Payment:	All Major, Check

UP STAIRS ON THE SQUARE
BED & BREAKFAST

320 Ranch Road 12
Wimberley 78676
Reservations: 800 949 9075/512 847 5300

Innkeepers:	Bruce & Dave Calkins
	Resident Owners
Open:	All Year
Facilities:	2 Bedrooms, All Private Baths
Breakfast:	Full
Rates:	$75 - $85 For 2 Guests
Payment:	All Major, Check

WIDE HORIZON BED & BREAKFAST

781 Sunset Drive
Wimberley 78676
Reservations: 512 847 3782

Innkeeper:	Sallie Arbogast, Resident Owner
Open:	All Year
Facilities:	2 Bedrooms, All Private Baths
Breakfast:	OYO
Rates:	$90 For 2 Guests
Payment:	Check

WILDFLOWERS RETREAT CENTER

P.O. Box 2173
Wimberley 78676
Reservations: 512 847 3083

Innkeeper:	Patti Brooks, Resident Owner
Open:	All Year
Facilities:	1 Bedroom With Bath
Breakfast:	Restaurant Voucher
Rates:	$95 For 4 Guests
Payment:	MC,Visa,Check

WILEY'S COTTAGE

15 Buttercup Lane
Wimberley 78676
Reservations: 512 847 7322

Innkeepers:	Mr. & Mrs. Wayne Wiley
	Resident Owners
Open:	All Year
Facilities:	1 Bed - 1 Bath Cottage
Breakfast:	Continental
Rates:	$75 For 2 Guests
Payment:	All Major,Check

WIMBERLEY

A short distance South of Austin, North of San Marcos, is the picturesque community of Wimberley, a resort and retirement area. Nearby is R. M. 12, a razor-backed ridge road overlooking Hill Country vistas, extending 24 miles West of Blanco, known as the "Devil's Backbone," one of the most scenic drives in Texas.

A popular visitor attraction is "Market Day" which is held the first Saturday of each month (and only on Saturday), April through December, at Lions Field located on Ranch Road 2325. Admission is free and parking cost is nominal. Acres and acres of shopping draws tens of thousands to this weekly event.

Another "must" for visitors is a stop at "Blue Hole" which has been in operation since 1928 and certainly a big part of Wimberley history for many years. It has been the backdrop for movies ("Honeysuckle Rose" and "Small Town in Texas") but more importantly has provided countless hours of relaxation and fun. "One of the top ten swimming holes in Texas" - you don't want to miss this unique experience.

Spectacular panoramic views are in store for those who climb "Mount Baldy" where you can even see the towers near Austin. This craggy, limestone mountain towering 1,182 feet offers some railings and a few plateaus for resting as you climb.

Birding in the area is also tops on the list of "things to do". Two endangered species, The Golden-Cheeked Warbler and the Black-Capped Vireo, have their habitats in the juniper shrouded hills.

# Winnsboro

THEE HUBBELL HOUSE

307 W. Elm
Winnsboro 75494
Reservations: 903 342 5629/800 227 0639

Innkeepers:	Dan & Laurel Hubbell
	Resident Owners
Open:	All Year
Facilities:	12 Bedrooms, All Private Baths
Breakfast:	Full -Mansion/OYO-Carriage Hse
Rates:	$75 - $175
Payment:	All Major,Check

Thee Hubbell House is located in the beautiful Northeast Texas town of Winnsboro. Located on a two acre plantation estate, it consists of four historical houses with a total of twelve bedrooms with private baths.

The plantation was built by Confederate Colonel J. A. Stinson in 1888. His oldest daughter married Governor Jim Hogg of Texas, and their daughter was the famous Ima Hogg. The land had owners like General Sam Houston and General Robert E. Lee's cousin.

Guests may choose to stay in one of the five rooms in the Mansion itself or in the Cottage or Carriage House. Common areas include a formal living room with piano and fireplace, dining room, spacious verandas and upstairs gallery, garden room and patio. All rooms are graciously furnished with antiques. There is also an antique and gift shop on the premises.

A full breakfast is served in the Mansion dining room at 9 a.m. Continental self-served breakfast is provided in the Cottage and Carriage House.

Smokers may use the outside verandas. Children are welcomed in the Family Cottage only. Pets utilize the Veterinarian Pet Motel. The inn is handicap accessible. Senior citizen rates are offered as well as extended stay discounts, business rates and special discounts for reserving the entire estate.

Directions: 90 Miles East of Dallas, I-30 to Sulphur Springs, then Southeast on #11.

Member: Texas Historical Association, Texas Hotel/Motel Assn, East Texas B&B Assn

# Wolfforth

COUNTRY PLACE BED & BREAKFAST
Upland Avenue
Wolfforth 79382
Reservations: 806 863 2030

Innkeeper:	Pat Conours, Resident Owner
Open:	All Year
Facilities:	5 Bedrooms, 1 Pvt Bath, 1 Shared
Breakfast:	Gourmet
Rates:	$70 - $100 For 2 Guests
Payment:	MC,Visa,Check

# Woodville

ANTIQUE ROSE BED & BREAKFAST
612 Nellius St
Woodville 75979
Reservations: 409 283 8926/800 386 8926

Innkeepers:	Jerry & Denice Morrison
	Resident Owners
Open:	All Year
Facilities:	3 Bedrooms, All Private Baths
Breakfast:	Full
Rates:	$75 For 2 Guests
Payment:	Check

Yoakum

OUR GUEST HOUSE BED & BREAKFAST
406 E.Hugo
Yoakum 77995
Reservations: 512 293 6473

Innkeeper:	Shirley Blundell, Owner
Open:	All Year
Facilities:	4 Bedrooms, All Private Baths
Breakfast:	Full
Rates:	$40 - $45 For 2 Guests
Payment:	Inquire

NOTES

REGIONAL INDEX

The cities in this book are arranged in alphabetical order. To assist you in locating Bed and Breakfasts within a particular area, thereby giving you several choices, the following regional breakdown may be of assistance. Several of the towns in this book are so small that they are not on most maps.

Abilene Area
Abilene
Haskell

Albany
Sweetwater

Austin Area
Austin
Elgin
Round Rock
Salado

Bartlett
Georgetown
San Marcos
Taylor

Big Bend Area
Alpine
Marfa

Fort Davis
Shafter

Bryan - College Station Area
Anderson

Calvert

College Station
Huntsville
Rockdale

Franklin
Navasota

Corpus Christi and the Costal Bend Area

Corpus Christi
George West
Padre Island, North
Rockport
Sinton

Fulton
Kingsville
Pettus
Seadrift
Victoria

Dallas Area and North of Metroplex

Argyle
Denison
Fink
Plano
Saint Jo
Van Alstyne

Dallas
Denton
Garland
Royse City
Sherman
Whitesboro

East Texas - North I-20 Area

Dangerfield
Mount Vernon
Paris
Sulfur Springs
Winnsboro

Mount Pleasant
Omaha
Pittsburg
Texarkana

East Texas - North I-30 Area

Avinger
Big Sandy
Edgewood
Gladewater
Karnack
Marshall
Tyler

Ben Wheeler
Canton
Emory
Jefferson
Longview
Mineola
Uncertain

Fort Worth Area and South of Metroplex

Bluff Dale
Cleburne
Fort Worth
Granbury
Teague
Weatherford

Corsicana
Ennis
Glen Rose
Stephenville
Waxahachie

Golden Triangle Area

Beaumont
Silsbee

Port Arthur

Hill Country

Bandera
Boerne
Burnet
Comfort
Fischer
Granite Shoals
Ingram
Kerrville
Lampasas
Mason
Quihi
Stonewall
Uvalde
Wimberley

Blanco
Buchanan Dam
Center Point
Dripping Springs
Fredericksburg
Hunt
Johnson City
Lakehills
Leakey
Pipe Creek
Rio Frio
Utopia
Vanderpool

Houston - Galveston Area

Conroe
Dickinson
Friendswood
Houston
Pasadena
Spring

Cleveland
Freeport
Galveston
Kemah
Seabrook

Houston to San Antonio - North of I-10

Bellville
Burton
Chappell Hill
Fayetteville
Ledbetter
Round Top
Warrenton

Brenham
Carmine
Columbus
La Grange
Paige
Smithville

Houston to San Antonio - South of I-10

Eagle Lake
Shiner

Gonzales
Yoakum

Lubbock and South High Plains Area

Crosbyton
Lubbock
Quitaque
Spur
Wolfforth

Floydada
Olton
Ropesville
Turkey

Mid to Far West Texas

El Paso
Odessa

Iraan

Panhandle

Amarillo
Canyon
Memphis

Canadian
Clarendon
Miami

Piney Woods Area

Alto
Crockett
Jasper
Palestine
San Augustine

Broaddus
Hemphill
Nacogdoches
Rusk
Woodville

San Angelo Area

Ballinger

Paint Rock

San Antonio Area

Bulverde
La Coste
Rio Medina
Seguin

Castroville
New Braunfels
San Antonio

The Valley
Harlingen
Padre Island, South
Rio Grande City

Linn
Raymondville

Waco Area
Eddy
McGregor
Moody
West

Hillsboro
Meridian
Waco

Wichita Falls and South
Archer City
Jacksboro
Wichita Falls

Eliasville
Seymour

ORDER FORM
CALL TOLL FREE AND ORDER NOW

Please send ____copies of
The Texas Bed and Breakfast Directory to:

Company Name: _____

Name: _____

Address: _____

City: _____ State: ____ ZIP: _____

Telephone: (____) _____

Sales Tax: Add 7.25% for books shipped to Texas addresses.
Shipping: Add $3 for first book
and 75 cents for each additional book.

FAX ORDERS: (713) 370 4446
TELEPHONE ORDERS: Call Toll Free: 1 (800) 231 1904
(Have your VISA or MasterCard ready)
POSTAL ORDERS TO:
Golden Pen Publishing Company
P O Box 73028
Houston TX 77273-3028

Method of Payment:
___ Check payable to Golden Pen Publishing Company
___ VISA ___ MasterCard
Card Number:_____

Name on Card: _____Exp Date: ___/____

Signature:_____

On Gift Orders we will ship direct with a card!
Message:_____